BERND DEGEN
DISCUS
A Reference Book

BERND DEGEN
DISCUS
A Reference Book

A pair of wild-caught *Symphysodon discus discus*. These are called Discus Heckel in the trade.

Distributed in the UNITED STATES by T.F.H. Publications, Inc., One T.F.H. Plaza, Neptune City, NJ 07753; in CANADA to the Pet Trade by H & L Pet Supplies Inc., 27 Kingston Crescent, Kitchener, Ontario N2B 2T6; Rolf C. Hagen Ltd., 3225 Sartelon Street, Montreal 382 Quebec; in CANADA to the Book Trade by Macmillan of Canada (A Division of Canada Publishing Corporation), 164 Commander Boulevard, Agincourt, Ontario M1S 3C7; in ENGLAND by T.F.H. Publications, PO Box 15, Waterlooville PO7 6BQ; in AUSTRALIA AND THE SOUTH PACIFIC by T.F.H. (Australia) Pty. Ltd., Box 149, Brookvale 2100 N.S.W., Australia; in NEW ZEALAND by Ross Haines & Son, Ltd., 82 D Elizabeth Knox Place, Panmure, Auckland, New Zealand; in the PHILIPPINES by Bio-Research, 5 Lippay Street, San Lorenzo Village, Makati, Rizal; in SOUTH AFRICA by Multipet Pty. Ltd., P.O. Box 35347, Northway, 4065, South Africa. Published by T.F.H. Publications, Inc. Manufactured in the United States of America by T.F.H. Publications, Inc.

CONTENTS

The first recorded spawning of *Symphysodon aequifasciata axelrodi* was accomplished by Gene Wolfsheimer. He also was the first to explain how baby Discus feed. His story appeared in *National Geographic* magazine.

Discus are so hybridized now that their origin is indeterminate. This specimen, for example, has the characteristics of both species of Discus.

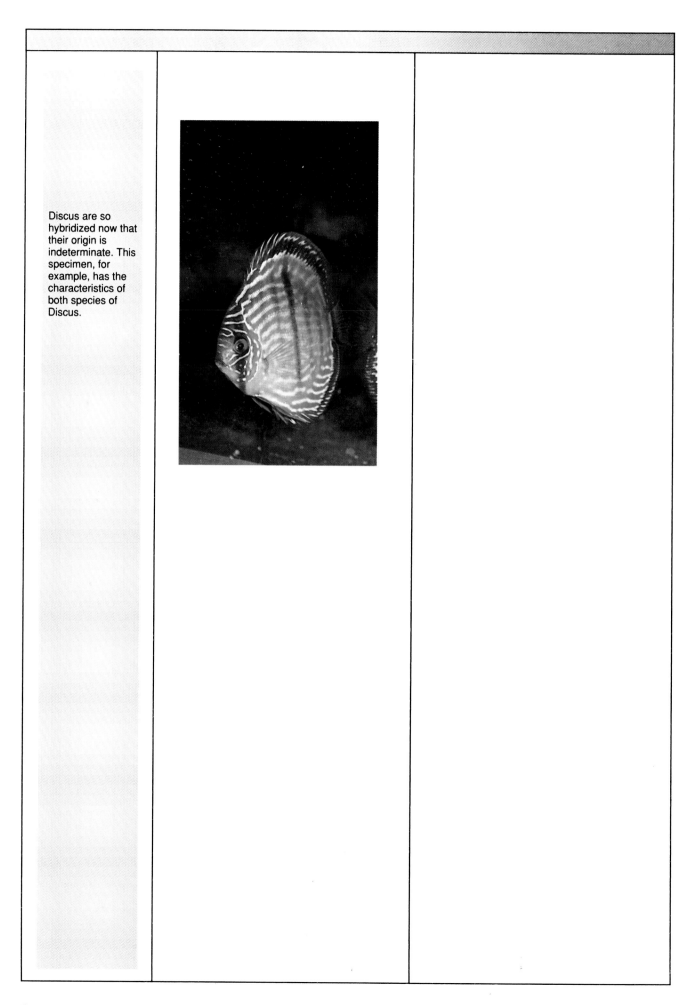

PREFACE

One thing I learned when I first started to write about Discus and my first couple of books were published: Discus fanciers are always looking for more good photos and information about their favorites. That is how the second edition of this book that you are reading came about. It will give you new information about the fish (the group of fishes, really, because there are a number of different species and subspecies all lumped under the name **Discus**) that is rightfully known as the **King of the Aquarium**.

It will also, however, give chapter and verse on keeping and breeding these fishes. Additionally, it is sufficiently comprehensive to ensure that more and more aquarists will turn to Discus of one type or another—or perhaps even to a number of different types at the same time. Once infected by Discus fever, there is no escape.

This book was conceived with love. I hope it will give you much pleasure and also help to secure the future of our Discusfishes in the aquarium. I hope, too, that the book will help you to get to know the Discus even better as a lovable domestic pet, not just as an aquarium inhabitant. They should eat out of your hand!

I should like to offer a note of appreciation to all of my Discus friends and acquaintances who have helped me in various ways while I was writing this book. Whether they wrote me a letter or spoke to

Bernd Degen, circa 1988.

me on the telephone, whether they discussed their method of doing things or let me photograph their Discus, I owe them a vote of thanks.

My special thanks go to my Discus friend Dieter Putz, with whom I spent many an hour in front of a Discus tank. Special thanks also go to Uwe Heinrichs for his fine photos and for his text about a beginner's first experiences.

And a big thanks also to all the photographers who sent me their finest Discus photos so that this book can show off some of the best—not only the most colorful but also the most shapely—Discus in the world.

Bernd Degen

FIRST EFFORTS
By Uwe Heinrichs

In the beginning, there was quite an unnatural respect for this true King of the Aquarium, the Discus. These splendid cichlids were always my dream fish as an aquarist. Now the dream was at last to become reality. Three Heckel Discus were the start. However, theirs was a dull existence in a well planted-up community tank with Neons, Angels, catfishes and a few other species. My joy with the Discus fish was short-lived with me, the same way it was with many other beginners. But now, ambition and curiosity for this new fish had me in thrall. To begin with, I read everything about Discus I could lay my hands on. The community tank was converted to a pure Discus tank with plants. The Angels and Neons had to go. I took time to set up the aquarium and to prepare the water, which was soon to accommodate my new treasures, five half-grown Royal Blues. Through careful, frequent feeding and regular partial water changes, problems in keeping were carefully avoided.

Now the Discus took hold. The tanks became ever more numerous and larger, the Discusfishes ever more splendorous—and, unfortunately, more expensive. No distance was too great for me to travel to obtain specimens of these fine fish.

Before long, my hobby was crowned by a 125-gallon (500 liters) tank in the living room, with eight adult Turquoise Discus. Had everything—really everything— been achieved? No, becuase I still had not yet spawned the fish, and before that happened a great deal of time was to pass and much money was to be spent on acquiring experience. When searching for suitable breeding pairs I soon found that this was a road set with snares and pitfalls. But even here, obstinacy was rewarded. My prize was a real pair of Turquoise.

After a fortnight, the fishes courted and spawned. Almost hour by hour I went to the tank to see how many eggs were fungusing. This is really a fearful time for the Discus breeder. I was lucky. Many fry hatched from the first clutch. But my luck was to be of short duration. The same evening the fry became free-swimming they suddenly disappeared. The solution to the riddle was the filter. It had simply sucked up the fry.

The next spawn was not long in coming, and this time everything ran to perfection. After five weeks I had fished more than 100 young Discus from the tank and transferred them to a rearing aquarium. Many broods were to follow. Today the Discus is no longer a mystery to me, but it is still the most fascinating of aquarium-dwellers and the fish that gives the attentive keeper the most joy.

A Cobalt Blue
champion Discus
feeding his fry.

FROM THEN UNTIL NOW

1840 is the magic date for the discovery of the Discus. The Viennese ichthyologist Dr. Johann Jacob Heckel described a specimen in Natterer's collection as *Symphysodon discus*. In Dr. Heckel's honor, this fish is still called the Heckel Discus in aquarists' references. It was not until 1930 that the first Discus were imported into Germany and the USA. Even then, only a few select aquarists had the opportunity to acquire them. Whether they succeeded in breeding them we do not know. All that subsequent reports say is that the Discus behaves much like the Angelfish in its reproductive capacity. That, too, was probably the reason why it still took so long before progeny were successfully obtained from the Discus.

In the early days of Discus keeping, eggs were actually taken away from the parent fish to protect them from the latter. Attempts were made to raise Discus artificially, as had already been done with Angels. William T. Innes, through his *The Aquarium* magazine, filled the aquarium world with incorrect information. He was aided by the people from Paramount Aquarium, whose obvious falsehoods about collecting Discus in a net were meant to discourage collectors. Their outright exaggerations about collectors being eaten by piranhas and alligators was further evidence of false reporting! Here are the actual articles which appeared in *The Aquarium* magazines of March, 1934; December, 1946; and June, 1948. By the way, Innes probably coined the term "King of the Aquarium."

Symphysodon discus Spawns

To Gustav Armbruster, of Philadelphia, goes credit for the first spawning of the Pompadour Fish (*Symphysodon discus*) to be brought to our attention. The eggs, unfortunately, proved infertile, but as the first step toward successful propagation of this colorful species, Mr. Armbruster's achievement seems to us to deserve mention.

Apparently the spawning habits of the *discus* differ but little from those of the *scalare*.

The colors displayed by both sexes of the *discus* during and prior to the mating were magnificent. The light tan background became a deep coffee brown, from which the blue and green markings on the head and body and along the base of the dorsal and anal fins shone out like opalescent fire.

THE AQUARIUM

for March, 1934

THE RETURN OF THE DISCUS

BY *Henry A. Nichols*

WE are at last approaching the day when rare aquarium fishes, so long absent from our collections, once more may be available to the lucky fanciers who can obtain them. To some degree they will be a little now than it could twenty years ago. After he reaches the airport nearest the stream in which he intends to hunt, the collector still must combat such matters as training and paying for native help, the avoidance of rampant tropical dis-

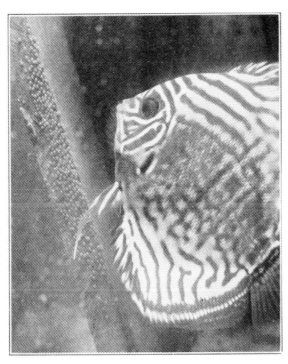

Male Discus Fanning Spawn

easier to obtain than they were in pre-war days, for shipment by air will result in the happy landing in northern lands of many fishes which could not withstand the relatively long journies by ship and railway. Nevertheless, the advent of the swiftest commercial stratoliners will still not render commonplace the truly rare Exotics. Before they are placed on the loading platform at an airdrome in one of the hot countries, they must be collected, and that cannot be done any more quickly or cheaply eases, protection against virulent insects and reptiles, and a few other matters that have no relation whatever to the miracles of modern transportation. All of which should be taken into consideration if a dealer asks a moderately high price for a selected pair of fishes.

One of the leading New York importing firms, the Paramount Aquarium, recently returned to the market one of the most outstanding of the rare exotic fishes—*Symphysodon discus,* the Pompadour Fish. Paramount's President,

[221]

Mr. F. Cochu, began last winter to lay his plans for returning to his old hunting-spots, in South America, from which some of our most beautiful aquarium fishes already have come, and where there undoubtedly are still more magnificent new species, still unrevealed. On Christmas Day of 1945, Mr. Cochu and his "old standby," M. Rabaut, left Florida for the Brazilian jungles in an ancient double-wing Clipper. They were sure, after a few hours, that they would never get back to New York alive, or, for that matter, even reach their intended base of operations. The plane had obviously never been designed for days over impenetrable jungles or the elevations of more than 12,000 feet that are required to cross the Andes. Finally, however, after some four days of flight, they located the Amazon about 1,000 miles upstream from the closest seaport.

First investigations revealed that virtually none of their old-time, thoroughly trained native helpers were to be found. The Piranhas and alligators had accounted for some of them. Others had followed a gold rush or moved off to the new rubber plantations that wartime demands had developed. Still others had succumbed to one of the myriad diseases that are virtually uncontrolled in that part of the world.

However, the two fish collectors finally got themselves organized, and, as Mr. Cochu puts it, they "fished and fished and eventually managed to catch about 10,000 specimens; some of each of a number of species, but nothing rare." But it was a start, and enough were brought safely home to cover expenses, and to announce to members of our hobby that importations were beginning to arrive again. The return trip was made in February, by air to Florida, and from there the fishes were

trucked to New York—at just about the worst time in the year to bring in a shipment of Tropicals. The greatest disappointment, of course, had been their failure to get in touch with their former native helpers, for it takes a long time to train wild men to hunt for non-edible fishes that are to be handled very carefully and moved long distances alive.

In March, Mr. Cochu returned once more to South America, and this time he went alone—not to fish but simply to try once more to round up sufficient of his experienced native fishermen. After travelling for a great many miles up and down a large number of jungle streams, he located a few of them, who agreed not only to come back to work for him, but to show unskilled fishermen how to hunt for aquarium Exotics for the New York market. This accomplished, Mr. Cochu returned to this country, stocked up with a good supply of collecting and shipping equipment, motors, medical and food supplies, etc., and went back to the jungle again—this time accompanied by two of his American assistants, Messrs. Kramer and Krause, who both were well acquainted with life in the great tropical jungles.

Starting off in different directions, the three men each made nice collections and finally met at a selected central point from which all were to move back toward an airport. Mr. Kramer, however, turned up with a raging fever and an injured leg, and he was forced to leave his collection behind him and fly at once to the United States for treatment. After several weeks he was quite recovered. Mr. Cochu, who has already departed on his seventh South American trip since the end of the war, tells us that he rarely makes such a journey without losing approximately twenty pounds, but that his wife's good care and nourishing food quickly return him to full strength again, after he gets home.

Speaking of *Symphysodon discus,* Mr. Cochu reports that when he was finally able to start hunting again for this beautiful aquarium species, he found that there were absolutely none in the waters where they had originally been trapped. There were a number of other species quite at home there, but not a sign of a Pompadour. He could not understand this strange disappearance, even though the fish had never been particularly plentiful, and he was getting extremely worried, when, one day, on a more or less aimless excursion up a small tributary to the great Amazon, he pulled in his net and found in it two fine Discus. He tells us that it was all he could do to resist jumping into the water to be sure to land those two safely into his boat. After a little more work in the same spot he caught six more, and then had to return to his camp for food. In that part of the world one can sometimes go a little while without adequate nourishment, but not for long, especially when doing any fairly heavy work. However, as soon as he had laid in a good stock of supplies. Mr. Cochu went back to his newly discovered Discus spot and caught 32 more, for a total of 40 fine specimens, all of which he was able to transport safely, and in perfect condition, to his hatchery in Ardsley, New York.

How many of these rare and beautiful fish Mr. Cochu intends to place on sale, and how many he may keep in the hope of breeding them, we cannot say. In 1934 one pair, owned by the late Gus Armbruster, a Philadelphia dealer, produced a number of large spawns, much in the manner of the Scalare. Only three of them hatched, however,

and of these only a portion of one lot could be saved for more than a few days, because it was apparently impossible to supply them with just the right infusoria, except on this single occasion. We are not sure, of course, but since the grown Discus has a notably small mouth for so large a fish, it seems possible that their fry require food considerably smaller than that taken by most other baby Cichlids. At any rate, Mr. Armbruster was able to grow 35 young Discus to fair size. Many fanciers then believed that it would be only a matter of time before later generations, produced from these tank-bred specimens, would become as plentiful and cheap as the Scalare. But that never happened. The big pair stopped spawning for keeps and not a single one of the youngsters ever showed the slightest interest in breeding.

Before the war, it was more or less a tradition that "Discus eat nothing except Tubifex Worms." The present specimens, however, readily accept Daphnia, *Enchytrae,* Ghost Worms and, in at least one case, infant Guppies— although the fish are so peaceful that they make no attempt to bother large Guppies and certainly could not swallow one. It may be that acceptance of a more varied diet will result in the present-day Discus being more fertile than were the pioneer stock. Moreover, Mr. Armbruster used to keep all of his fishes at a very high temperature. That is excellent for forcing growth, but it undoubtedly results in shorter life and, quite possibly, in decreased fertility as well. We shall await with interest such reports as may come in on the current crop, and perhaps this time some lucky aquarist will determine a way to bring true that great dream of all fish fanciers—"Tank-raised Discus, guaranteed mated pairs."

SYMPHYSODON DISCUS (HECKEL)
Still King of the Aquarium

BY *William T. Innes*

AFTER the first several importations there followed a number of years in which no more "Discus" were brought in, largely due to the effects of World War II.

For some time now Paramount has been bringing them in, but in most ways the fish is as much a mystery as ever, but in one respect it remains the same in the eyes of many fanciers. It is still "the King of the Aquarium." To those who like their fish large and showy, this certainly fills the bill, and it is still rare enough to command attention wherever it is seen.

There is one difficulty that has been overcome to a certain extent. The first importations got off to a bad start when they reached this country. This was in the matter of their food. They were given Tubifex, and as this was evidently a luxury, they soon got so that they would not consider anything else, and owners were slaves to getting this tidbit, *or else.* We now know that if they are allowed to get a little hungry, they will take other foods that agree with them, Daphnia and White Worms in particular.

As was proved by Armbruster, who raised the first batch, they really can be brought to eating ordinary aquarium foods, especially if started young on the routine. He reared about 33 of them, and they ate just like any ordinary aquarium fish, but were not spoiled by getting Tubifex except as an occasional luxury.

Much study was given to finding a definite means of telling sex. Several times the question was thought to be solved in various ways, but the best recent opinion is that the majority of all specimens are females. The males are much more covered by the blue pattern, while the females, in addition to having less blue, also develop a golden-yellow background as breeding time approaches. This is sometimes very pronounced. The male in breeding color equals in brilliance any of the tropical marine fishes. The blue irregular stripes extend nearly all over the body and into the dorsal and anal fins in such a way that it is impossible to tell where the body ends and the fins begin. Much of the space between the jagged stripes becomes a glowing, deep cherry color.

Our plate gives a fair idea of the difference in color at breeding time. What has already been said will probably enable the reader to select the sexes of a pair.

The species, being Cichlids, spawns in the usual Cichlid manner, with few exceptions. After various flirtatious movements in a clumsy-coy manner, accompanied by appropriate oglings of eyes, the pair lock lips, front to front, taking a firm hold, which they maintain for short periods. Between kissings they back off and seem to threaten each other. Then one dashes forward, apparently bent on a battering-ram attack. At the last instant a collision is avoided by a slight change in direction, and a side movement by the still fish. In each instance observed the pass was made to the right. They evidently observe American traffic rules!

[119]

A short egg-laying tube, or ovipositor, appears from the vent of the female a day or two before spawning. With this she places the eggs, a few at a time, in close, neat rows. They are of an amber color, and slightly elongated. The male follows immediately after his mate and fertilizes the eggs with spermatic fluid ejected from a tube similar to that of the female. In both sexes the tubes disappear within a week after spawning is finished.

Various objects have been tried as a base on which the fish might deposit their adhesive eggs. As a bar of slate was successfully used in one of the early instances, this material has since been utilized. The size of the bar is about 1/2 inch thick, 2 inches wide and 16 inches long. This is stood at a sloping angle against the glass in the tank.

Although the parents exhibit the keenest of interest in the eggs, taking turns fanning them with their pectoral fins, the sad fact is that after 2 days or so they eat either eggs or the newly hatched young. Repeated experiments have proven that parents and eggs should be separated after a day. A needed mild circulation about the eggs and young is produced by a nearby outlet of air liberated in the water.

Various hatching temperatures have been tried. The first successful one by Armbruster was at about 85 degrees. Recently we were again thrilled by a successful second breeding. This was by the Paramount Company, of New York, and we understand that they also used a high temperature. This was 13 years after the Armbruster hatching, but a larger number of the young were safely brought through — 56, to be exact.

The mouths of the newly-hatched young are extremely small, and the great difficulty seems to be to find infusoria that are the right size and which will live at a high temperature. Armbruster evidently struck on the right combination purely by luck, for he was never able to repeat, even though there were numerous spawnings from the same pair, which hatched after being removed from the parents.

AGE 2 MONTHS
Dorsal fin dull red.

We recently made inquiry at the Paramount Company as to the first food used. Their reply is that they used 5 different kinds of infusoria, hoping that one of them would answer the purpose. They do not know which one proved successful, but we may depend upon it, it was one of the smaller kinds, and yet it had to be sufficiently meaty to prove nourishing.

Here again history repeats itself, for there was no subsequent successful spawning, and in the meantime the pair of breeders died from abscesses in the head, produced by a parasitic worm to which this species is subject. This is being studied by Dr. Nigrelli with the view to discovering a remedy, and we can only hope that he will come up with the answer, as he usually does.

The illustrations used herewith were taken from the Armbruster breeding, but they are still applicable. A quick glance at them shows that growth is rapid. Color changes have been few. When at the smallest size shown, the dorsal fin was a dull red, nearly all over. The 8 bars gradually darkened, especially the one through the eye. Flashes of characteristic metallic blue developed later in the dorsal and anal fins. In the last picture it can be noted that the ventral is more pointed than previously.

It should be noted that the Armbruster breeding occurred in a 60-gallon tank containing slightly acid water, and the eggs were then placed in a small aquarium in a depth of water not over 3 inches. This was continuously aerated so as to produce about the same water current over the eggs as the parents would have made in fanning them.

The most beautiful pair we ever saw was owned by Mr. Franklin Barrett, and at that time the male was fanning eggs on the broad edge of a slab of slate. He disregarded our advice to separate the eggs and the parents, with the result that within another day every egg was eaten.

Ordinarily this fish does not fight, except occasionally with its own kind. When the eggs have been removed by their owner, each seems to blame the other for the loss, and there is liable to be expensive trouble. For the sake of safety, following the removal of eggs, the pair should be separated for at least a week, by the use of a glass partition.

There seems to be no general rule as to whether the male or the female does the attacking. With the successful breeder pair they took turns at it, each becoming the aggressor on alternate days. As flower pots and vigorous plant growths furnished good refuge for the pursued, the owner for a few days allowed Nature to take its course, but finally became alarmed and divided them by a partition. After a short enforced separation, all was peace again and no trouble was experienced when they were placed together. On the other hand, Mr. Barrett had one female kill

3 males. As the males are the more valuable, she has been an expensive fish to him. *Symphysodons* never attack other species, and seldom its own.

AGE 3 MONTHS
Most of red has disappeared from dorsal fin.

It is rather tantalizing to know that the fish has been bred successfully, and yet we are not able to unlock the secret that would unable us to do it consistently. Incidentally, the fellow who succeeds, if he is a professional or semi-professional, will have a private gold mine.

AGE 4 MONTHS
The 7 body bands, instead of their usual dark color, were light when this photograph was taken.

Only in the 1960s did the first real information about Discus fish reach the aquarist journals. At the same time, the airline connections with the fish-collecting stations in the South American jungles were improved. It then became possible to send fish worldwide from Iquitos in Peru, Leticia in Colombia and Manaus and Belem in Brazil. The range of Discus was soon broadened, and this paved the way for the boom in wild-caught Discus during the 1970s. It was then the basis was laid for the quality fish available on the market today. Discus are the kind of fish that tireless breeders have spent long years raising to a standard of quality that surpasses anything that came before. From fish generation to fish generation, the colors have been more strongly highlighted, while still largely retaining the typical Discus shape, so that today we have Turquoise Discus, in particular, that are at about the pinnacle of their potential development.

Gene Wolfsheimer, a California fish breeder and photographer, was the first person to photograph a whole spawning cycle of Discus and to discover and explain the theory of babies feeding from their parents' bodies.

THE HOME OF THE DISCUS

Discus range over a wide expanse of rainforest in northern South America; rivers in which they live can be found in at least four different countries: Brazil, Colombia, Venezuela and Peru.

The rivers are divided into three types, depending on the kind of water; there are white-water, black-water and clear-water areas. The best known and largest are the white-water rivers of the Amazon, including the Solimoes, the Rio Madeira and the Rio Branco. Important clear-water rivers are the Rio Tapajos and Rio Xingu. Black waters are found in the Rio Negro, Rio Abacaxis and Rio Cururu.

White-water rivers with turbid, loam-yellow water offer visibility of only a few inches. These white-water rivers carry rich sediments to the Amazon. The silt is transported from the Andes right down to the Atlantic. This white water has a pH value of just below 7. Its conductivity, at 30 to 60 microsiemens, is still the highest of all of the water types.

Because of the large quantities of deposited matter that these rivers carry with them, their banks undergo continuous change.

Black-water rivers are colored an olive to dark brown and are rather more transparent. Visibility is possible to depths of 5 ft. (1.5 m). Their conductivity, at 10 to 20 microsiemens, is very low, and the pH value, too, is low: at between 4 and 5, it's at the bottom end of the

A scene found throughout the Amazon River system. Boats are repaired, stored and sold here. Fishermen are eager to "hire out" with their boats and crews to collect Discus for the Yanqui.

The area in the Rio Tefé where Dr. Axelrod discovered the Green Tefé Discus.

scale.

Clear-water rivers, with their greenish color, have the highest transparency. Here, visibility has been measured to depths of about 4 yards (4 m). Like the black-water rivers, the clear-water rivers also have an unfavorably low electrolyte content; their conductivity is less than 15 microsiemens. The pH value is usually between 5 and 6.

Huge areas of the Amazon are flooded each year during the rainy season. These floods offer the fish good spawning conditions in newly created shallow waters. High water temperatures produced by the strong sunlight on these small ponds encourage the Discus to spawn. At the same time many infusorians appear, which together with all of the other types of tiny water animals offer the young fish

an abundance of food. In these waters, to which the trees' shade does not extend, temperatures may rise to 90 degrees F. (32 degrees C.) so that the Discus enjoy ideal conditions for spawning. This knowledge can also be usefully applied to our Discus aquariums.

The heavy rainfall in the Amazon area starts in December. The rivers then reach their highwater levels in January and February. Floods occur and continue until June. The lowest water levels occur in October and November. The Discus are caught in the narrower backwaters of the Amazon during the rainy season. The main period for exporting wild-caught Discus is October to March.

Catching Discus is heavy work. The traditional method using a fixed net demands a good deal of preparation and work afterwards.

The trees have been cleared from the water and the net circles the Discus in the Rio Urubu in Brazil. Several hundred Discus were collected in one net after a whole day's work.

The Rio Purus at Tapaua. Cardinal Tetras and beautiful Discus are found in this river.

The nets are staked out while the area enclosed is freed of fallen trees, driftwood, roots and branches. Once this heavy, laborious work has been done, the nets can be pulled in to obtain the rewards of the labor. Catching Discus at night is also popular. The fish are then sought with a strong spotlight or flashlight, dazzled and gathered in. The enormous cost of fuel, for both aircraft and boats, has had a detrimental effect on Discus catching.

The European market is also at a disadvantage, as many Discus from the Amazon basin are sent to the United States. The world market for wild-caught Discus has clearly deteriorated in recent years since so many healthier and cheaper tank-raised Discus are available.

Turquoise Discus feel secure with the plants in the background. The slightest scare and the fish dash headlong into the plants. Sometimes, when they are very frightened, they will dash into the glass and kill themselves accidentally.

Did you ever see a pair of fish in love? This is about as close as fish can come to being in love. Discus mate forever. They stay mated unless one of the fish dies. They swim together and stay next to each other most of the time. Unfortunately, this pair is not similarly colored, but their intense mutual devotion made it impossible to separate them. Love conquers all.

The black Rio Negro meets the brown Rio Amazonas outside of Manaus, Brazil. This is called the "Marriage of the Waters."

Local fishermen use thrownets to capture fishes near grassy marshes. They occasionally capture small Discus in these areas. These small Discus have been expelled from the family hideaway because the parents were getting ready to spawn once more.

Discus are stored in floating or stationary net traps awaiting the fish buyer who comes every few weeks to collect the Discus from hundreds of such stations. Dr. Axelrod set up this system in 1952 when he was in the business of selling Discus and Cardinal Tetras from the Rio Negro.

Plain Cobalt Blue Discus. This male with the hump on his forehead (because he is old) would be more ideal if he were solid blue cobalt without any body markings.

DISCUS TAXONOMY

There are only two species of Discusfishes (five separate taxa, as one species encompasses three subspecies), but those two species have managed to generate a tremendous amount of taxonomic confusion among ichthyologists and tropical fish hobbyists alike.

The Discus lover distinguishes between four types of wild-caught Discus. First of all is the Heckel Discus, or Pompadour, scientifically known as *Symphysodon discus discus*. This fish is immediately recognized by its thicker fifth body stripe. The first and last of the vertical stripes, too, are more strongly marked. Because of these strong markings, the fish has not been propagated in hobbyists' aquariums. Today few, if any, home-bred Heckel Discus can be found on the market. Progeny with these vertical stripes are

simply unsaleable. Dr. Axelrod discovered another Heckel Discus subspecies, *S. discus willischwartzi*, in the Rio Abacaxis. It is similar to *S. d. discus*.

Heckel Discus have very fine base colors, which may vary from reddish to turquoise blue. Thickset wild-caught specimens with a strong blue cast are a feast for the eyes. Crosses with Heckel Discus are therefore popular, especially in Asia, to retain the blue or turquoise lines in the progeny. Attempts to breed away the vertical central stripe have not been entirely successful. Heckel Discus are sold as Pompadour Discus, Blue Heckel and Red Heckel. The Rio Abacaxis Discus have not been bred to date. They are too rare and expensive.

The name Brown Discus refers to *Symphysodon aequifasciata axelrodi*. This wild-caught Discus

This is the modern look in Discus. Really good quality Turquoise Discus are the basis of the Discus-breeding industry of the 1980s. The 1990s are featuring more intensely colored Discus.

was the one most frequently found in hobbyists' tanks in the 1960s and 1970s. It is practically the ancestor of our present-day Discusfishes. Its basic body color is a light to dark brown. It has a few blue stripes on its head, back and vertical fins. The anal fin usually includes fine red markings. Blue stripes occur above the eye and are more strongly marked on the anal fin.

Brown Discusfish with a strong reddish cast in the green are often called Red Discus, but this morph occurs only infrequently. No home-bred specimens of the pronouncedly Red Discus, whose basic color is red instead of brown, are known. Young fish, especially those from

Asia, which are offered as Red Discus have been colored through the use of special food. The color disappears when this food is no longer fed.

As with all other wild-caught Discus, the color of the eye may proceed from red through orange to yellow. Discus breeders usually go for fish with red eyes.

Another Discusfish is the Green Discus, *Symphysodon aequifasciata aequifasciata*, also commonly sold as the Pellegrin Discus. The fish was classified by Pellegrin in 1903. The ordinary Green Discus has a greenish-brown base color, with green stripes around the back and stomach. Fish striped all over in

Do they look related to you? These are the two basic species of Discus. The Brown Discus represents the subspecies *Symphysodon aequifasciata axelrodi*. The fish with the wide bar in the center of its body is *Symphysodon discus discus*. It is called the Heckel Discus because Heckel was the scientist who first described *Symphysodon discus* in 1840 from specimens collected in the Rio Negro.

green or turquoise are known as Pellegrin Discus or, nowadays, also as Royal Green Discus.

A further green variant is the Tefe Discus. The striking features of the Tefe are its first and last vertical bands, which are strongly marked, and numerous red spots that are distributed all over the body, especially on the stomach. These fish are greatly coveted and at present still very difficult to obtain.

The turquoise-colored progeny have been raised from sturdy, well marked wild catches and are now standard. In Europe, in particular, the turquoise-colored offspring dominate the market.

The final type of Discus is the Blue Discus, *Symphysodon aequifasciata haraldi*. In its base color it is strongly akin to the Brown Discus. The fish is purple, especially in the head region. Blue longitudinal stripes cover the head, back and stomach. Its over-all appearance is most colorful and striking.

When fish colored blue all over were caught, they quickly acquired the name of Royal Blue. For years they were leaders in the Discus sector. Royal Blues have been and are the epitome of the super-Discus. Today, fine specimens are rarely found in captivity.

The powerful turquoise blue of these wild catches has been retained in their descendants. Homebred specimens are also now available under the name of Cobalt Blue. The ideal in this case is the solid cobalt blue turquoise fish, which is a glossy blue all over. The metallic

sheen never fails to fascinate the observer.

The forms of Discus are the ancestors of our homebred varieties. One of our tasks must be to maintain the typical discus shape and the stocky appearance of these fish. With a good round shape and a fine color, it matters little whether the fish comes from a Blue or a Green Discus. What is important is that the type should not be lost. Large-eyed Discus with gleaming colors but stunted growth aren't worth producing.

Fashionable colors and fantasy markings, repeatedly advocated by certain breeders, are bound to be short-lived. When turquoise-colored Discus display a touch of red in their basic coloring, the error of immediately offering them as Red-turquoise Discus must be avoided. Discus colors depend greatly on the angle of light as well as on water quality, food, the general condition of the fish and other factors. Photos of the same specimens taken shortly after each other soon prove this. The slightest changes in the light will change the picture completely.

Names such as Albino Discus, Electric-blue Discus, Cobalt Discus, Ghost Discus, Peruvian Green Discus, Gypsy Discus, Red-pearl Discus and Spotted Blue Discus have come and gone in quick succession.

Dr. Axelrod collected this strain of Green Discus with blood red eyes in Lake Tefé. The fish he brought back alive formed the basis of fancy Discus breeding in the 1960s. His Purus Discus (illustrated on page 30) completed the inventory of blue and green *Symphysodon aequifasciata* which produced most of the fancy hybrid varieties known today.

This is the Royal Blue Discus which Dr. Axelrod collected with Willi Schwartz in the Rio Purus. According to Axelrod, only dominant males had this color. Fish like this are the standards by which other fish are measured.

BRINGING THEM BACK ALIVE

Tank-bred Discus provide a larger portion of the total captive Discus population every year, but wild-caught Discus are still a significant part of the trade.

The golden age of wild-caught imports is undoubtedly past. In vain, many dealers wait for larger quantities of the fine wild-caught types since, after all, the magnificent Royal Blue always found a ready market. Since 1983 the quality of imported wild catches from Brazil has clearly deteriorated. Ordinary brown and green catches are relatively easy to find, while Tefe or Royal Blue specimens are virtually unobtainable. Prices, too, have naturally risen, which may ultimately be ascribed to inflation, the increased cost of fuel and the fact that collectors have to travel farther and farther from their home bases in order to catch fish.

The important stations are in Belem and Manaus (Brazil) and Leticia (Colombia). There, the Discus that are caught are collected and held for export. As these fish mean good money to the exporter, special efforts are made to keep them in good health. They are prepared for transportation in large plastic containers or tiled tanks. It is important that the fishes' intestines should be empty, since excrement in the water during transport can produce dramatic changes in its quality. The fish, therefore, are not fed for several days before despatch. They are then packaged

In 1957, Dr. Herbert R. Axelrod went Discus-hunting in the Rio Negro. He hired local fishermen, like the ones shown here. The fishermen came with their wives and children to meet Axelrod. The wives stayed around the mother boat (the *Ebenezer*) and had a chance for a rare visit with each other. The children played in the shallow water. Suddenly the children screamed—one had been attacked by a huge catfish. The women grabbed harpoons, which are always kept around for killing stingrays. They harpooned the catfish and took the child's legs from its mouth. Here is the family and the dead catfish. The family had a big party afterward, eating the fish. The Indians are very afraid of these huge catfish, and many legends tell about the mysterious disappearance of fishermen gobbled up by these scaleless giants.

The author, Bernd Degen, checking the water chemistry of the Rio Negro.

in a double plastic bag, the larger and medium-sized specimens being packaged individually. The transport bags contain just enough water to cover the fish in a vertical position. With added oxygen in the bags the fish will tolerate transportation for 48 hours. To avoid fluctuations in temperature the bags are placed in thick expanded polystyrene boxes that are carefully sealed. The fish then set off on their long journey in these insulated containers.

When you consider that the fish are packaged several hours before departure and must then be taken to the airport for the customs clearance formalities, that the flight generally takes 10 to 20 hours, that customs takes up a further 2 or 3 hours and that transport to the dealer's tank must also be included,

it is not unusual for them to spend 36 to 48 hours in transit. Added to the stress of this long journey is the yet-to-come long haul to the hobbyist's tank.

If imported by a wholesaler or large importer, the fish are first accommodated in the importer's installations. From here the road continues, soon after if possible, to the tanks of the nearest wholesaler and retailer. Once the fish slowly begin to adjust to their surroundings and to eat properly again, the hobbyist comes along as the last link in this chain and carries the fish to his home aquarium. This, for the time being, is the end of the line.

If the fish has successfully survived so far and we retrace our steps a little, we can see that a wild-caught specimen will usually already have spent four to six weeks in captivity before ending up in a fancier's aquarium. During this period it has encountered at least three total water changes and a long phase of inadequate food supply. It then becomes the aquarist's task to nurse the fish back to health and help it recover its full beauty. It goes without saying that the keeper of these wild-caught specimens needs some flair and love for his hobby. Wild catches should therefore be left to the more experienced aquarist.

The newcomer is advised to try his luck with healthy home-bred fish, which need not necessarily be inbred Turquoises.

Many thousands of young Discus are now exported to Europe from Asia, especially from Hong Kong, Bangkok in Thailand and Singapore. Jamaica and Trinidad also export Discus; these Discus are sent to the United States almost exclusively.

The quality of the water in Hong Kong, Bangkok and Singapore is ideal for the Discus breeder. It is very soft. In Hong Kong, for example, the pH value is generally over 7 and is reduced for breeding purposes. Gigantic daily water changes of 50% and even more offer the fish ideal conditions for breeding and growth. Because of the daily water changes, no filters are used at all. The breeding pairs sit in a small tank often containing only 22 gallons (80 liters). The tank contains nothing apart from a spawning cone or piece of slate.

Live food is present in

The most successful collector of Discus is Dr. Herbert R. Axelrod. He spent 40 years collecting more than 24 different Discus varieties in the Amazon and Rio Negro rivers and their tributaries. Here, in 1989, he is returning on his famous Brazilian boat, the *Ebenezer*, sleeping during the day in a hammock and fishing during the night. The deck of the boat is covered with plastic fish boxes.

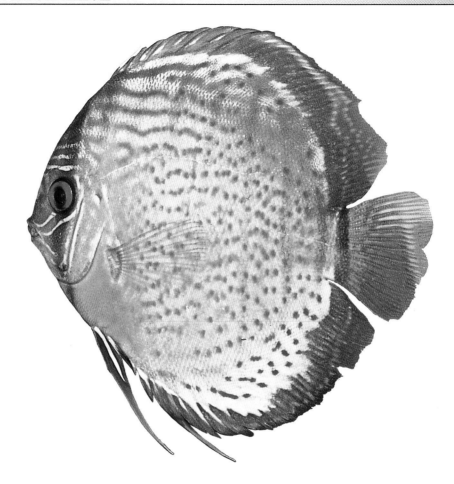

The red dots on this fish indicate that it is wild-caught. The variety is from the Tefé area of Brazil.

abundance, though the type of food differs from one country to another. Tiny water fleas, known as "dust Daphnia" are offered to the Discus fry. Apart from tubifex and mosquito larvae, various species of freshwater shrimp are also featured in the diet. An important food are the eggs of the local crustacean *Macrobrachium rosenbergi*, which grows to some 7 in. (18 cm). The red-colored eggs contain a great deal of carotene which when fed to the fry quickly produces a reddish coloring. Of course, the young Discus lose the red hue when the food is withdrawn, so these fish should not be sold as Red Discus. Most young fish from Asia are descended from Brown and Blue Discus. Heckels, too, are repeatedly crossed in. Unfortunately, good breeding specimens are rare, so quality home-bred progeny are still valued highly abroad.

Unfortunately, the lighting was poor for this photo of two really great Brilliant Turquoise Discus. This is a well-matched pair. The male, in the background, is slightly larger than the female. Both are inbred for brilliant turquoise color and have similar colors and markings.

CURRENT STATUS

Some fanciers are only casual Discus owners, but there are others who are devoted—almost dedicated—Discus owners. Among the first group are those countless aquarists who generally purchase young specimens in the local pet shop because they like the look of the fish. They perhaps believe that young Discus are a worthwhile purchase because they are something special and will turn into fine fish in due course. They will no doubt have to tolerate some losses among their Discus if they keep them in a community tank. They will, however, try again and perhaps even a third time. At some point they give up keeping Discus. A few will learn from their mistakes, go in for Discus more intensively and set up special Discus tanks. Then, undoubtedly, their efforts will one day prove successful; these aquarists will then join the second group, among whom I number the readers of this book—a not exactly small group of Discus lovers who have become devoted to this fish. Once infected by the Discus "bacillus" they can be counted among those aquarists who know how to keep Discus successfully and perhaps even persuade them to breed.

Discus breeders who for various reasons have reached near-professional standards in breeding remain a fringe group. But even here there are distinctions. Some of these breeders pursue their hobby because it is a challenge. The sale of successfully home-bred fish raises just enough money to cover their expenses. Perhaps now and again they earn a little from it, but when we include the work put in, the account drops back into the red. Professional breeders have already turned to mass production, most of them trying to meet certain quality standards. These breeders generally sell their progeny to wholesalers, but sometimes to private people as well. The main object must, however, be the sale of whole broods at the age of six weeks. Here, large-scale sales are required. Home-bred Discus are now sold in large quantities in Continental Europe, Britain and the USA.

Unfortunately, still far too few quality progeny reach the wholesalers and retailers. A shortage persists, because the market demands quality specimens that are healthy and stable. There is undoubtedly still a market here for Discus breeders. Small home-bred specimens 2 to 2.5 inches (5 to 6 cm) in length are easily obtained. Medium-sized fish 6 to 8 months of age are harder to find, although they have every advantage.

With such fish the purchaser will be able to judge the coloring, the body shape and the general appearance of the fish. And, of course, the price will still be worthwhile. If the fish are diligently kept, the purchaser will have viable breeding specimens after only a few months.

Mature adult specimens with good or even very good coloring are very difficult to obtain. Even where such fish are advertised, the

A solid, healthy male Brilliant Turquoise circa 1985. Specimens bred in 1991 were solid color green blue turquoise.

The fish above and the two fish below are the same subspecies, believe it or not! The pair below come from the Belem do Para area of the Amazon, close to the Atlantic Ocean, while the fish above came from around Santarem. These fish were imported in the 1960s.

reality is rather different.

Discusfishes are not easily raised. Because of their size, Discus already restrict the raising potential from an age of six months or so. These fish can be quarrelsome, and aquariums containing a dozen of them will be the scenes of struggles for power and territory. If the fish are to be raised from that point to a still larger size, at least 8 to 13 gallons (30 to 50 liters) of water must be allowed for each fish. It should now be clear why so few adult fish appear on the market. What's more, a hobbyist who has

taken the time and trouble to raise good specimens will be unwilling to sell them again. Once he eventually has a dozen large Discus in his own tank, he will want to set up pairs and produce successful young Discus of his own.

Among Discus lovers, only quality specimens with good coloring can be sold. The color trend in recent years has clearly been toward the Turquoise Discus, striped specimens being especially favored. Turquoise Discus with solid turquoise coloring are rather scarce and are still the exception. Also available are Red-turquoise Discus, though this calls for a word of warning. The composition of the water, i. e., its iron content, may influence the coloring of the Discus. It has been found that specimens with a pronounced red proportion in the basic coloring began to lose it in the new owner's tank; this loss of coloring resulted from the composition of the water.

Other hues play a subordinate role. Ordinary Brown or Green

Discus are no longer saleable— or at least, aquarists have become so demanding that they still want only Turquoise specimens. Even beginners keep away from home-bred Browns. An adult Brown Discus, however, can be the centerpoint of an aquarium. Between green plants and large bogwood roots such a fish can be a king.

The number of Discus lovers is increasing all the time. The quality of our home-bred fish must therefore remain the supreme aim for serious discus breeders. Home-bred specimens must retain the sturdy, thickset, round shape of the Discus. If the color gradations have also been successfully reproduced to the previous quality, the wild-caught varieties can largely be ignored, as is the case with other animals such as the carp and the goldfish. After all is said and done, ignoring the wild-caught fishes and concentrating only on those that have been bred domestically is good for the protection of the species and preservation of the biotope.

This kind of *Symphysodon discus* was said to come from the northern Rio Negro around the Rio Içana, but several collectors were unable to verify the truth of the statement.

A beautiful young fish with nice color and nice form.

This fish was starved as it grew up. Already too old to recover, it will be skinny, feeble and sad looking all its life. In nature such a fish would have been eaten by predators early in its life. In the aquarium, it can live for years. This is the result of underfeeding during the fish's first few months.

THE BEST IN THE WEST

The well known American Discus breeder Jack Wattley often travels to Germany to visit discus-keeping friends. As a result of these visits he has on more than one occasion taken German-bred fish back with him to the USA. Discus bred in Germany are very popular world-wide. Today, many of these small Discus go to Belgium, Holland, Great Britain, the USA, Canada and even Japan.

In Germany, a number of Discus breeders began (in the early 1980s) to raise Discus in large numbers. As a big potential for very nicely colored fish was available, large numbers of quality young reached the hobbyist market. The Royal Blue and Turquoise varieties soon led the field. These color varieties, especially the Turquoise, are now bred in volume, making it often seem more difficult to obtain good home-bred Browns than young Turquoise.

As a result of years of purposeful breeding, Discusfishes in general have acquired colors of an intensity not found in nature. Selective breeding, a service performed by our Discus pioneers, has achieved this standard. The real difficulty in present-day breeding is that parent fish used for this purpose have the color but no longer the traditional round shape of the Discus. Elongated Discus are becoming more and more frequent. These fish are often affected by damage caused during growth. Fortunately, damage of this kind is not inherited, so we can be certain that an impaired parent fish will not pass it on. The growth of small Discus is soon impaired beyond recovery if they are taken ill during the first months of their lives. The breeder must therefore pay particular attention, especially in the first six months, to the growing Discus. Provided Germany can maintain the existing standard of quality, there can be little doubt that she produces the finest Discusfishes.

The truly serious Discus breeder can insist upon receiving a certificate which attests to the age, color and size of the fish on a given date, as well as identifying the breeder. Certified Discus are available from aquarium specialists only. Don't expect to walk into just any aquarium store and get pedigreed Discus...but they can be ordered by your local aquarium dealer through mail order ads in *Tropical Fish Hobbyist* magazine.

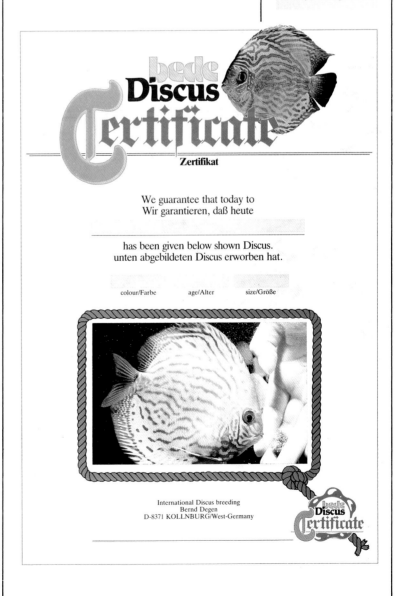

bede **Discus Certificate**

Zertifikat

We guarantee that today to
Wir garantieren, daß heute

has been given below shown Discus.
unten abgebildeten Discus erworben hat.

colour/Farbe　　　age/Alter　　　size/Größe

International Discus breeding
Bernd Degen
D-8371 KOLLNBURG/West-Germany

bede Discus Certificate

BASICS OF MAINTENANCE

Healthy young Discus at the age of six weeks crowd around a food tablet. At this age they are growing quickly, and the Discus must be fed five or six times a day. Live foods, frozen foods and dried foods must be alternated. Actually, food tablets are not good for Discus because they usually contain excessive amounts of heavy metals. Freshly frozen or clean live foods are best.

Somehow over the course of time people in the aquarium hobby have had it drummed into their heads that Discus are touchy and temperamental and difficult to keep. It so happens that the Discus is a problem fish only because people say it is. So-called Discus specialists have steadily built up the myth of breeding difficulties and problems in keeping them. Discus fall ill only if they are kept wrongly and inattentively. The Discus are tougher and more long-lived than most ordinary pet fishes.

Of course, there are rules to be observed when looking after Discus to make sure that the fish remain healthy and bright.

The most important instrument the keeper has at his disposal is the water. In nature, Discusfishes live in extremely soft water. However, this water contains many organic substances that are of vital importance to the Discus. On the other hand, if we put too many organic substances into our tank water it will turn brown and turbid, which detracts from the appearance of the fish. No Discus-lover will want to see his fish swimming in a thick brown soup. It is, therefore, advisable to keep them in medium hard water of approximately 10 to 15 degrees of German hardness. The hardness should be reduced for breeding, though peat extracts, trace elements and multi-vitamins will be added.

The pH value of the aquarium

water also requires particular attention. For keeping purposes, all values between pH 6 and pH 7 will do. What must be avoided at all costs is a sudden change in the pH value caused by the use of acidifying agents.

Using acids can have catastrophic consequences for the fish even if only a small error is made. The pH value may sink sharply, especially when the water is very soft. Slight corrections of the pH value may be made by filtering the water over peat.

A slightly acidic environment should be aimed at for breeding. Once again, though, the pH value should not fall below pH 5. Breeding water acidified with peat also benefits the eggs laid. The bactericidal effect of the peat is unquestionable and prevents fungus from forming on the eggs.

The Discus keeper must watch the water temperature very carefully. The Discus likes warm water. Ideal keeping temperatures are 84° - 86° F. (29° to 30° C.). Temperatures below 82° F. (28° C.) must be carefully avoided. If you want to do your fish a favor, the temperature may from time to time be raised slowly over the course of a day to 88° to 90° F. (31° to 32° C.) and then allowed to drop back to normal on the third day.

Changes in water temperature also stimulate egg-laying. The fish can be stimulated to courtship and egg-laying through a change of water, with rather colder or warmer water added to the tank. The beneficial effect of this stratagem of course depends on having the fish ready for spawning before the water change is made. And of course in the case of adding cold water the idea is to add only enough to *stimulate* the fish, not shock them. Stimulation can lead them to spawn; shocking them will lead only to sickness.

As it is exremely difficult to protect fish against bacterial attack in small aquariums having a proportionately small volume of water, it must again be stressed that the best means of preventing bacterial attacks is partial changes of the water. If the tanks are over-populated or if too little water is changed, the nitrate and nitrite content in the water will necessarily rise. As stated, these toxins can be removed by changing the water or by installing ion-exchangers.

The exchanger resins regulate the pH value at the same time, adjusting it to a level of between pH 6 and 7. Make sure, however, that you use an exchanger resin which leaves the organic substances in the water.

Of course, whether a Discus feels at home depends greatly on the food it is given. As we shall largely be keeping only tank-bred specimens, we can forget about the

Brown Discus, *Symphysodon aequifasciata axelrodi*, and Heckel Discus, *Symphysodon discus discus*, together with Cardinal Tetras, *Paracheirodon axelrodi*, highlight a nicely furnished community aquarium.

eating habits of the wild varieties. In nature, Discus fish prefer to feed on freshwater crustaceans.

Variety is the key to feeding. It goes without saying that the fish must be offered a selection of various kinds of food. If fish are given one kind of food only, it is hardly surprising that the females will not show a tendency to spawn. The standard Discus foods include

control. The substrate in particular conceals hazards. Food residues easily settle in the gravel and foul gases develop. Bogwood roots, too, may introduce decay in the water and start to make it smell bad. The build-up of nitrites and nitrates then soon reaches a level harmful to the Discus. The fish turn dark and stick to one corner of the tank. At that point the aquarist should take

A good spawning, successfully raised, should number about 80 fry at about one month of age. These Brown Discus, *Symphysodon aequifasciata axelrodi*, are good examples.

not only the dry prepared foods such as the flake foods, but also, especially, beefheart and enchytraeid worms. When the beefheart and the worms are further enriched with vitamins and minerals, there is little more the fish could wish for.

Many Discus are kept in aquariums without substrate and furnishings. However, there are some aquarists who prefer to see their Discus in planted-up and fully furnished tanks.

In tanks of this kind, the quality of the substrate and of the roots introduced must be kept under strict

suitable steps. One solution, for example, is to cover part of the tank bottom with gravel. The glass bottom is left exposed in the front of the aquarium while a layer of gravel and aquarium plants is built up at the back. Tanks of this kind are easily cleaned and still look good. If the Discus-lover observes these rules he will have already avoided many problems.

TO BREED OR NOT TO BREED

Whether a hobbyist thinks about it when he acquires his first Discus or whether he doesn't think about it until after he's had some experience with them, sooner or later he'll ask himself: should I try to breed my Discus? This is even more true with Discus than it is with other fishes, because the fact that the Discusfishes are cichlids means that their brood care is interesting and delightful to observe. Watching a brooding Discus pair must be the greatest pleasure an aquarist can have!

The Planted Discus Tank

One of the first things that must be decided is whether the Discus tank is to be planted or not. That is, we must decide whether the fish are to be kept in a planted aquarium or in a Discus tank without further furnishings. In the former case, the plants must be selected with the Discus in mind.

When selecting the plants we must also remember that Discus can be kept only at temperatures that are considered to be too warm for a number of plants. Unfortunately, you cannot make compromises here, as Discus kept in water that is too cool will soon become ill.

It is by no means easy to reconcile plant and fish requirements in this case with a successful display aquarium as the end result.

Effective growth of water plants requires a tank with a suitable

substrate. As water plants must be properly provided with natural iron, the bottom layer of sand should be mixed with an iron-containing substrate. The installation of substrate cable heating should also be aimed at so that the plants do not get cold root; a heated substrate also improves the circulation of the water. A natural flow of water is created along the bottom of the aquarium; this flow benefits the plants and enhances the continued stability of the substrate. To my knowledge, this practice of using a heating cable to warm the plant roots is almost purely a German innovation; perhaps it deserves a more universal adoption. Heating cables keep outdoor water supplies of dogs, chicckens, etc., from freezing.

The prepared sand layer is covered with a further layer of gravel, consisting only of washed stones. A harmonious picture is

If you cannot tell the difference between a good quality Discus and a "pet" quality Discus, you should not be a Discus breeder. Begin with good quality stock. It takes as much time, effort and expense to breed good quality Discus as it does to breed poor quality Discus.

This series of photographs shows typical Discus spawning behavior. A pair of Discus similar in size and color is set up for spawning. Both are 16 months old. The male is the larger of the pair.

The male Discus has accepted the pottery cone as his spawning site. This is indicated by his cleaning of the cone. Cleaning of the spawning site always precedes actual egg deposition. Usually spawning takes place within a day after the spawning site has been prepared.

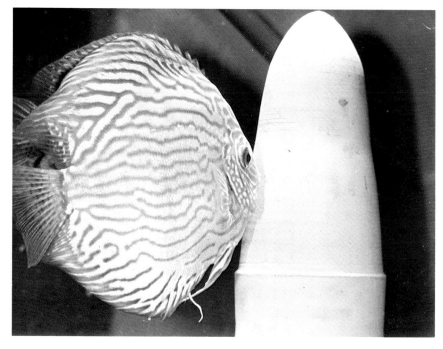

The female begins to lay her eggs on the selected and prepared spawning site. The black bars on her sides become more and more obvious. The other dark areas, such as the black on the unpaired fins, also become darker as the female "soots" herself.

Spawning commences with the female laying one row of eggs after another. After each pass, the female moves away and the male fertilizes the eggs just laid. Actual spawning usually takes about an hour, after which the parents alternately fan and guard the eggs.

created for the observer if the gravel rises slightly toward the back of the tank.

Discusfishes also like shelters and markers when forming their territories. Stones are especially suitable, but they should not make the water hard. Lava, granite and slate are suitable for this purpose.

Particular caution is required with bogwood roots, as they introduce problem-causing substances to the water. In fact, many a discus disease in the aquarium can be cured simply by removing the roots present in the tank and changing the water.

Excessively dense vegetation can easily have a negative effect. The

This beautiful aquarium featuring many plants and different kinds of fishes suits the Discus well, and they are therefore encouraged to spawn.

Facing page: The top photo shows Floating Water Lettuce, which keeps the strong top light away from the Discus and is therefore to be encouraged in aquariums which receive too much light. In the lower photo, the dwarf cichlid *Pelvicachromis kribensis* makes a suitable companion for Discus in heavily planted aquariums.

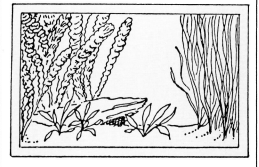

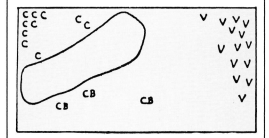

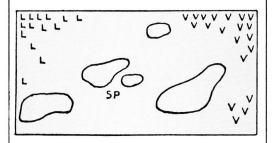

fish hide among the plants; they consequently become timid and are lost from sight. Following a planting plan is, therefore, advisable whenever a new tank is set up—but don't forget that water plants grow and reproduce. You have to take that into account in your planting plan.

For the vegetation plan, a sketch must be prepared showing all the plant locations. In a Discus tank, the vegetation will necessarily look somewhat sparse to begin with, but as the plants grow, appearances will improve (usually within two months.) There is no cutting corners with the quality of water plants. Only true water plants must be purchased. A number of attractive plants are available through the trade which are well suited as bog plants for growing above water, but once immersed they cease growing and soon perish. Plants with deep or varied colors should, in particular, be avoided.

The more important plants that have proved worthwhile in setting up a Discus tank are listed here for your guidance. For foreground planting, select species that have a low height Solitary individual plants give the Discus tank the necessary depth without letting the fish hide too much behind them. Tall and slender species are preferable for the background.

The Aponogetons and Crinums

Plants of the genus *Aponogeton* are suitable for all Discus tanks, as they tolerate temperatures of around 82 degrees F. (28 degrees C.). All species of the genus *Aponogeton* have corms and need a period of rest. In the aquarium they grow for six months or so and then begin to contract. The corms must then be removed from the aquarium and kept for several months in a cool place in wet gravel or damp peat. After resting for two months they should be returned to the aquarium, where they will again quickly grow into fine plants.

Aponogeton crispus

The narrow, lanceolate leaves are waved and slightly ruffled at the edge. The plants need plenty of light but then grow excellently. They readily flower in the aquarium.

Aponogeton henkelianus

This species grows very easily and makes no demands. As a solitary specimen it is the centerpoint for every aquarium. It grows to a height of 20 inches (50 cm).

Aponogeton ulvaceus

A tender, transparent plant, but still robust enough for the Discus tank. Its lush light green catches the eye. It can grow to more than 24 inches (60 cm) tall but generally stays smaller.

Aponogeton undulatus

A fast-growing plant with strong, olive-green leaves. It is particularly suitable for background group planting.

Crinum natans crispus

A bulb plant with narrow dark

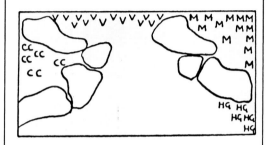

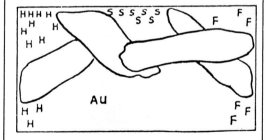

On these facing pages are four front views and layouts which may serve as suggestions for your own plans. The abbreviations are as follows: **AU:** *Aponogeton undulatus;* **C:** *Cabomba;* **CB:** *Cryptocoryne beckettii;* **CC:** *Cryptocoryne cordata;* **F:** *Ceratopteris;* **H:** *Hygrophila;* **HG:** *Eleocharis;* **L:** *Ludwigia;* **M:** *Myriophyllum;* **S:** *Sagittaria;* **SP:** *Echinodorus intermedius;* and **V:** *Vallisneria.*

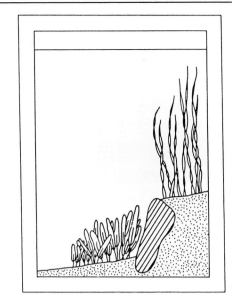

A cross-section of an aquarium in the planning stage, showing the use of small plants in the foreground and tall Corkscrew Val in the background.

Cryptocoryne balansae. The withered leaf shows how the leaf disintegrates in the aquarium when it gets too MUCH light.

green, knotted leaves, essentially curly and wavy. Owing to its extraordinarily shaped leaves it is an attractive display plant and also especially recommended for solitary planting. Because of its compact, leathery leaf structure your fish can do it little harm. In the aquarium it grows up to 20 inches (50 cm).

Crinum thaianum

A water-lily growing from a bulb. The species grows up to 40 inches(l00 cm). Its long, band-like leaves then float on the surface, where they form a natural cover. They should therefore always be planted toward the back and in corners.

The Cryptocorynes

Plants of the genus *Cryptocoryne* have strong, broad leaves and fit well in the Discus tank, where they provide ground cover. However, they should not be planted too densely, as regular cleaning of the substrate will be difficult. All Crypts grow very slowly and make specific demands on the quality of the substrate. They easily tolerate temperatures recommended for the Discus aquarium.

Cryptocoryne affinis

A well known species of Crypt with a sturdy habit. The upper side of the leaf is dark green, the other side reddish. These plants produce many shoots and will quickly spread if they feel comfortable. As they grow to only 6 inches (15 cm), they are suitable as foreground plants.

Cryptocoryne balansae

This Crypt has narrow, strongly knotted, greenish-brownish leaves. It needs plenty of light but makes no other demands. It can grow up to 16 inches (40 cm) and is suitable for middleground planting.

Cryptocoryne ciliata

Under good lighting *C. ciliata* grows up to 20 inches (50 cm). A fine solitary plant reproducing by runners. A group of three to four plants at the back of the tank is also to be recommended.

Cryptocoryne parva

A species of Crypt that remains extremely small. It grows to only 2 inches (5 cm) and is therefore particularly suitable for foreground planting to form a carpet. The fine, lanceolate leaflets are sharply pointed. They grow very slowly but steadily.

Above: The common Amazon Swordplant, *Echinodorus paniculatus.* Below: *Echinodorus cordifolius.*

The Swordplants

Plants of the genus *Echinodorus* generally are referred to as swordplants. They are bog plants from South America. *Echinodorus* species are commonly found in the aquarium, and are nearly all well suited to the Discus tank. Given a nutrient-rich substrate they respond by good growth. The genus includes both tiny dwarf plants for foreground planting and gigantic display plants. The species listed here tolerate water temperatures of up to 86 degrees F. (30 degrees C.), which predestines them for our Discus tank.

Common Val,
Vallisneria spiralis.

Echinodorus amazonicus

Sometimes popularly called the Small-leaved Amazon Swordplant, this species has spear-shaped light green leaves on short stems. Placed in groups, they grow to 14 inches (35 cm). On their own they can reach heights of 20 inches (50 cm).

Echinodorus cordifolius **The Cellophane Plant**

A majestic plant, often the centerpoint for large aquariums. It grows up to 20 inches (50 cm) and has light green, roundish to heart-shaped leaves that can achieve diameters of up to 8 inches (20 cm).

The plant tends to adapt to the size of the aquarium. Strong-growing floating leaves must be removed immediately.

Echinodorus muricatus **The Horizontal Swordplant**

A plant similar to the Cellophane Plant but with tapering leaves. The light green leaves are sometimes spotted brown. The plants grow fast and reach 24 inches (60 cm), at which point they may project over the edge of the aquarium. It then forms an attractive display plant, but the keeper must be prepared for this eventuality.

Echinodorus paniculatus

This is one of the best-loved of the swordplants and grows well. Its soft green, lanceolate leaves grow to 3 inches (8 cm) across. Large solitary plants form bushes with up to 50 leaves. Several of these plants set in the background are the right backdrop for a Discus tank.

***Echinodorus grisebachii* Dwarf Amazon Swordplant**

Many aquarists will be familiar with this dwarf swordplant. It forms a carpet in the foreground and grows to a height of only 4 inches (10 cm). It sends out runners that quickly form dense foreground vegetation.

***Echinodorus tenelleus* Junior Amazon Swordplant**

Growing to only 2 inches (5 cm), this is a true dwarf among the Amazon Swordplants. It grows best when given adequate light. With its runners it forms an attractive dense carpet of green in the aquarium.

The Vallisnerias

Plants of the genus *Vallisneria* are slender, decorative background plants that make no special demands as to aquarium water. They also tolerate temperatures of up to 86 degrees F. (30 degrees C.).

***Vallisneria gigantea* Giant Vallisneria**

Growing up to 80 inches (200 cm), this plant does full honor to its name. The strap-shaped leaves grow to 1.5 inches (3 cm) across, turning over as they reach the surface. It sends out many runners and reproduces well. A decorative background plant if placed in groups of three to five specimens.

***Vallisneria spiralis* Common Vallisneria**

The light-green thin leaves reach about half an inch (1 cm) across.

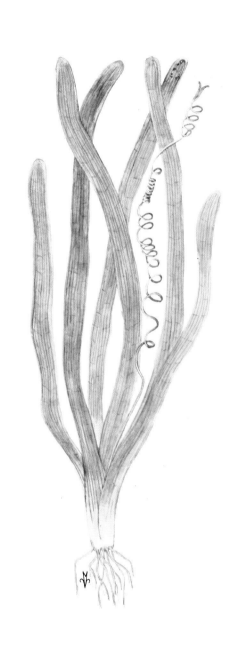

Giant Vallisneria, *Vallisneria gigantea*.

Vesicularia
dubyana, Java
Moss, growing from
a piece of driftwood.
This plant is very
decorative for the
Discus aquarium.

The spiralis part of the plant's scientific name comes from the flowering stems of the female plants, which grow in spirals. It also sends out many runners and grows very strongly. This species reaches 20 inches (50 cm).

Other Plants
Vesicularia dubyana Java Moss
An aquarium plant that prospers, covering stones and decorations with its dark green mossy carpet. It does not need a great deal of light.

The aquarium plants listed are a selection of ideal water plants for a Discus display tank. If the plants are to prosper, not only the substrate but also other factors must be taken into account.

Allowances must then also be made for the demands and living habits of the Discus themselves.

Lighting For The Plants
As water plants suitable for Discus tanks come from the tropics, they nearly all need plenty of light. Twelve hours a day is the ideal period. A sufficent amount of fluorescent lighting is needed for a water depth of 20 inches (50 cm). Optimum reflection of the light is achieved by a reflector above the tubes, too much light otherwise being lost. We must also remember that some fluorescent tubes lose up to half of their strength after six months.

An alternative to the fluorescent tube is the mercury vapor lamp or the halogen lamp. This is freely suspended above the aquarium, which must then no longer be covered. This means that the water plants can then grow out of the aquarium, thus creating a very special visual effect. When selecting the lighting and setting up the aquarium, some rather darker corners must be left for the fish to which a Discus can then retire. It is quite wrong to say that Discus like only dimly lit and dark aquariums. After all, in nature they are exposed fully to the tropical daylight.

Once the aquarium has been planted for Discus it must be given an opportunity to break itself in. The aquarist must be generous in this case and allow at least two weeks—or preferably even four weeks—before introducing his Discus to the tank. As algae are prone to emerge in a newly set up plant aquarium, algae-eating fishes should be installed from the start. From four to six Chinese Algae-eaters (*Gyrinocheilus aymonieri*) and three to five *Otocinclus* catfishes are suitable for an aquarium holding 50 to 75 gallons (200 to 300 liters). These fishes should not be fed during the first two or three weeks so that they can concentrate on devouring the algae. A few armored catfishes, *Corydoras*, can be introduced later to clear up food scraps.

Above: An *Otocinclus* catfish which removes algae from the aquarium glass, gravel and wood. To the left is a *Corydoras aeneus* catfish which scrounges about the sand searching for bits to eat.

COMPATIBLE SPECIES

Whether a Discus display tank needs any other fishes at all should be carefully considered, because not too many other species do well with Discus.

Angels will certainly not do, as these predatory eaters snap up much of the food ir.tended for the Discus and also introduce parasites. If you really want to keep other fishes in company with your Discus you should concentrate on a school of Amazon tetras such as Glowlight Tetras, Cardinal Tetras, Rummynose Tetras, Black Neon Tetras, Ornate Tetras, Rosy Tetras, Serpae Tetras or Neon Tetras. As all these species are schooling fishes and are seen at their best only in quantity, at least ten should be kept together in a group. In large tanks, a pair of Rams, which are of course particularly peaceful, can accompany the Discus. The focus of the tank, however, should always be the Discus themselves.

Serpae Tetras, *Hyphessobrycon serpae*, may be kept with Discus.

Rams, *Microgeophagus ramirezi*. These are very peaceful dwarf cichlids.

The Cardinal Tetra, *Paracheirodon axelrodi*, is the favorite fish to be kept with Discus because it lives in the same waters in the Rio Negro and Rio Purus.

Glowlight Tetras, *Hemigrammus erythrozonus*.

Black Neon Tetras, *Hyphessobrycon herbertaxelrodi*.

CHOOSING THE RIGHT DISCUS

Discusfishes are not mass-produced. True, every month several thousand young Discus fish are sold in Germany and elsewhere, yet certain basic rules must be observed by the potential purchasers.

Discus should be bought only where the purchaser can be sure that he receives the fish he is being offered. If he buys Turquoise offspring, Turquoise is what should be swimming in his tank a few months later. After all, there is no way of telling the potential color of small Discus that are only six weeks old and 2 inches (5 cm) long.

It is always worthwhile to catch one in a net and hold it up against the light. Take a good look at it. Even at this age, the color of the scales will already tell you what morph you have. Even small Turquoise Discus must show an iridescent greenish color. The true Turquoise sheen must be visible right across the body. Not simply the head color but the whole body must be examined. This method also holds good for large fish. As lighting plays an important part in the brilliance of Discus coloring, the existing colors will be properly seen when the fish is removed from the water. In another tank, under better lighting, a previously unremarkable fish will display its full beauty. The time of day and the condition of the fish also play a part. The fish are particulary good in the evening hours. They will also put on their full finery if they are healthy and feel at home.

Discus fish must be round. The correct body shape must be visible even in the young fish. Elongated Discus have stunted growth. This impairment evidences itself in the form of enlarged eyes. If the eyes seem too large compared with the rest of the body, the fish has not grown properly. It must have been ill at some time and refused to take food for a while. This damage is already beyond repair. Even when very well kept, damaged fish will not grow back into shape.

However, the defect—fortunately—is not inherited. All that misshapen Discus fish pass on to their progeny are their natural, inborn features. Damage caused by human hands during raising and keeping is not passed on to the young. If the progeny are looked after well, they will attain the normal sturdy Discus shape and differ quite clearly from that of their parents.

When buying young fish, you must take particular care that they do not have knife-edge backs. Seen from the front or from above, the knife edge will be clearly visible. Young Discus whose head and back sections have receded in this way are beyond recovery and unsuited for subsequent breeding. Seen from the front and from above, the head section of a healthy Discus must be clearly rounded outwards, the shape of the head being round especially above the eyes.

Buying Discus takes time. An observer sitting quietly in front of a tank for several minutes will soon

Here are two magnificent Turquoise which are almost identical in coloration. They can be expected to produce offspring very similar to themselves. Matches like this are to be desired so that good characteristics can be genetically fixed.

zG

The holes and ruts in the gill cover of the Discus on the facing page are normal and should not be considered as a manifestation of hole-in-the-head disease.

see what is wrong in it. Caution is necessary if the fish are timid and hide in a dark area of the aquarium. Healthy Discus also show their vertical stripes, as these are signals used during battles for territory. Visible vertical stripes indicate that there is nothing wrong with the fish's health. If, however, the fish are completely dark and the color does not quickly return to normal, it is better not to buy them. Healthy Discus produce reddish brown to black excrement, depending on the food. Large lumps of excrement in the water or hanging from the fish may be an indication of their health. Whitish, transparent, and gelatinous strings of feces indicate an infestation with parasites. These parasites can certainly be dealt with, but the new owner must know how to go about it. Newcomers to Discus-keeping would do better to try their luck elsewhere.

Many Discus fish have small holes around the head. Why this should be so is difficult to say. As *Hexamita* has so far not been discovered in Discus, we must assume that the holes are the result of attacks by a spironucleus or other causes. Small holes the size of a pinhead around the eyes may be regarded as harmless and normal; they are probably a sign of aging, although such holes are found even in yearlings. Larger crater-type holes, on the other hand, are more serious. Discus with large, unsightly holes may be suffering from hole-in-the-head disease. If white lumps or growths appear in the holes on the head, the fish should not be purchased.

A further point that requires the attention of a Discus purchaser is the gills of the fish. Discus suffer easily from gillworms and other gill parasites. Fish infested with parasites or worms commonly breathe on one side only. This means that only one gill cover is spread for breathing. The second cover.is held close to the head. Rubbing of the gill area against items of aquarium furniture also indicates infestation. Gillworms or parasites are a nuisance; they make life hard for the Discus. The problem can be cleared up with medications, but the new owner will have to spend some time treating the fish. This also presupposes that a quarantine tank is available, as the fish must first spend two weeks in quarantine before they can be put together with other fishes already present.

As the purchase price for Discus is always relatively high, the purchaser may be well advised to observe the fish at feeding time. The well-being of adult specimens, in particular, which may easily cost more than a week's pay, must be checked in this way.

The fish should show interest in the food offered. They are peaceful eaters who like to take their time. If they are healthy they will select something from the food offered. However, they should not be fed too much before a potential move, as the water may then be polluted during the lengthy journey. They may disgorge food already taken when being caught.

The fish can be transported without oxygen over short

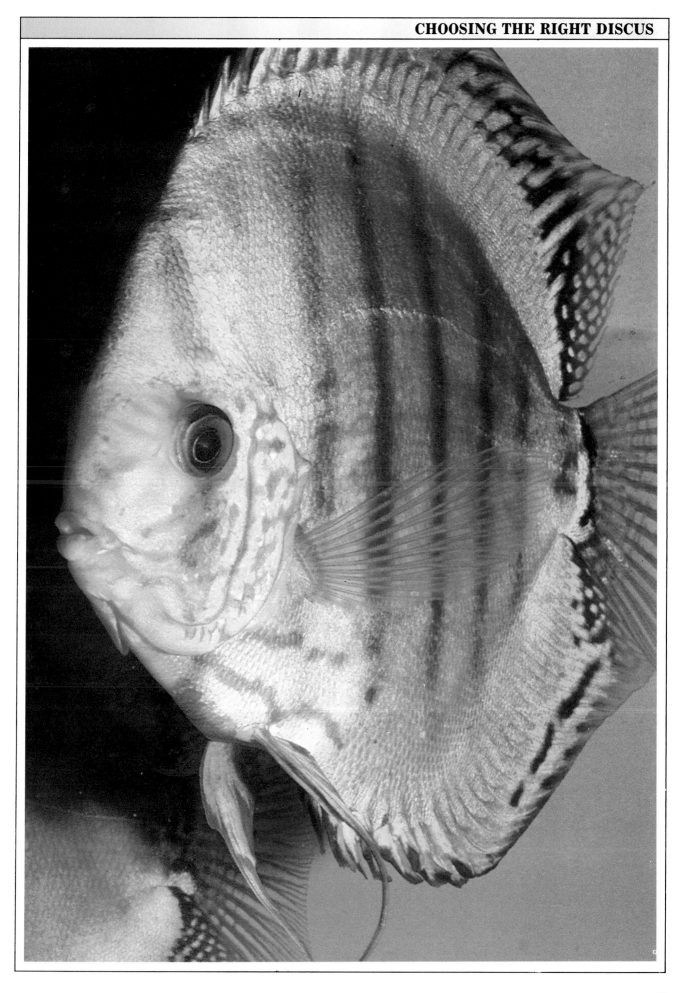

Even young fish 15 weeks old already show their body proportions. This will be a high-bodied fish, but its bulging eyes are discouraging.

distances. However, the amount of water must be adjusted according to the length of the journey. The longer the journey, the more water must be used. The safest way of transporting them is in a plastic bag that is placed in a carton. The cartons can be well padded with polystyrene or paper. Larger fish can make holes in plastic bags, so at least two bags should be used, one inside the other. Never carry unbagged Discus directly in polystyrene boxes or plastic buckets. The fish are timid and may easily be injured against the hard walls.

Damage to the membranes of the eyes can be acute in such cases. Once damaged, eyes usually stay that way. The pupil wastes away and remains small.

Peroxide tablets should not be used because, if given in the wrong quantities, they may prove detrimental to the mucous membrane of the fish. Pure oxygen from a bottle is ideal. With pure oxygen, the fish can happily withstand 36 hours in insulated polystyrene packs.

Transfer to the new home aquarium must be undertaken carefully. The tank water should be poured slowly into the carrier bag. The temperature and pH value should have adjusted within half an hour. The new fish can now be carefully removed with a net. The carrying water should be thrown away.

Large Discus at first adapt very poorly to the aquarium. They sometimes even lie flat on the bottom. They breathe very heavily, and their eyes bulge from their sockets. These symptoms, however, are no cause for a major panic, since within an hour (all other things being equal, of course) the fish will have begun to feel much happier in their new home.

The fish should not be fed during the first day. Small Discus, on the other hand, very quickly regain their appetites and should be fed sooner.

These are all brothers and sisters. They may be allowed to pair off and produce offspring similar to their parents and themselves. The larger fish are males.

CHOOSING THE SPAWNING PAIR

As important as it is to choose good Discus for normal aquarium conditions, it's even more important to choose the right fish to breed. Breeding attempts *must* start out with good specimens. What is required is a good, high-backed shape and keen colors. The round, thickset discus shape, in particular, should be retained in the progeny. Too much cross-breeding of different color morphs should be avoided. While it is true that inherited features are established by selective breeding, selective breeding presupposes that the breeder has sufficient space for an adequate number of fish that have the desired features.

To start with, a number of young fish may be procured. Because of possible inbreeding, however, fish from more than one pair should be raised for subsequent breeding; young from two pairs would be good, and three pairs would be even better. As it is not easy to raise young Discus without incurring some damage, sufficient young must also be kept available for this purpose. This means that the aquarist who seriously intends to build up his breeding stock should raise at least twenty and preferably thirty or forty young.

With the space normally available, it is of course difficult to raise forty Discus at a time. Raising that many is not strictly essential, but the greater the number of young available the more

This young Discus, only ten weeks old, is already showing fine coloration on its way to becoming a Green Turquoise.

opportunity there is for selection. After four to six months the young will have grown to 2 to 3 inches (5 to 7.5 cm) and will have already begun to display fine colors. Their body shapes and sizes must be carefully examined with a view to determining their sex.

The time has now come for making a selection.

Half the fish can be earmarked for further breeding. The selection criteria are the incipient colors, the body size, and the body shape. The young that do not come up to expectations completely should be given away. When selecting specimens by body size at this stage, care should be taken to ensure that in addition to the largest of the young an equal number of medium-sized young are also retained for further keeping. Experience shows that among siblings the females are rather smaller than the males. If only large specimens are retained, it might result in a surplus of males at a later date. The best specimens are therefore selected from the original thirty or forty. First attempts at spawning will be made by the time the fish are about a year old. However, the fish must be placed in smaller groups of three or four for this purpose. The fish will not readily form breeding pairs if kept in groups of ten or more in the aquarium.

Excellent pairs can be formed from the best fish obtained in this way. When forming pairs, an attempt should of course be made to get two specimens that both show the desired markings.

Unfortunately, it sometimes happens that ideal pairs will not tolerate each other; breeding then becomes impossible. Because of this, it is easy to see why a relatively large number of fish with similar markings should be kept. Only then is specialized breeding possible. Specialized breeding is different from ordinary breeding in that in the former case particular attention is paid to establishing the color and the pattern of markings.

The appearance of the 'brand' on the body, for example, is important. Fish whose lines run as parallel as possible are put together in order to establish this marking in the progeny. Or the high proportion of red in the ventral or pectoral fins should be retained and strengthened. When selecting the colors, fish with especially good depth of color should be combined.

If a strongly blue-colored plain Discus can be persuaded to breed, the young are bound for the most part to be similarly plain and powerfully blue. These features possibly can be increased further by backcrossing.

A Discus breeder who wishes to apply himself seriously to specialized breeding and inbreeding in order to produce first class specimens must devote himself intensively to the theory of inheritance and invest a great amount of time. As the quality of Discus can be assessed only after they are several months old, selecting specimens for continued breeding is a time-consuming job.

The rewards of this arduous breeding work can be seen in the

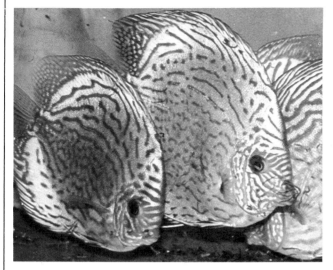

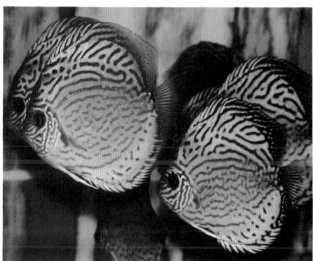
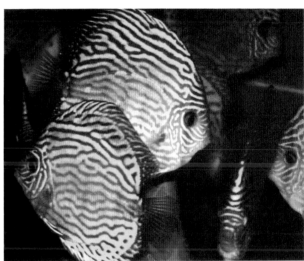

beautiful Discus swimming in hobbyists' tanks today. These fine fish have been developed from the natural forms. When comparing even the finest wild catches with Cobalts or Brilliant Turquoise, we must admit that such concentrations of color simply do not occur in nature. Careful selection and color breeding for years on end were needed to produce these results.

Nature has provided a fine Blue Discus, *Symphysodon aequifasciata haraldi*. Man has selected a few of the finest from hundreds of these wild catches in order to breed Royal Blue Discus, Brilliant Discus and Cobalt Discus

from them. Success has been achieved partly through mutations but partly only through stringent selection.

The Red Discus is now the dream of all breeders, but this will still take some time to achieve. The base material exists, but many factors play a part in this. It is unlikely that solid red specimens will be bred, even though Turquoise Discus with red cross stripes are already on the market. Turquoise Discus with brownish-red stripes cannot simply be offered as Red Turquoise. Where this happens, it is usually more a case of wishful thinking by the breeder.

Here are four examples of correct selective breedings. The groups are of Brilliant Turquoise, Red Turquoise and Striped Turquoise. The groups have been matched by color and sex.

This is a double catastrophe. A Brilliant Turquoise male Discus has been mated to a common Green Discus. He is much larger than she and never should have been paired with such an ugly fish (ugly by comparison to him). On top of this, the eggs have all turned white, which means they were not fertilized or were deficient in other ways.

DISCUS GENETICS

Discus breeders, in common with breeders of other species, in many cases don't pay much attention to the study of genetics as it applies to their Discus. If a pair forms and spawns and then diligently brings up the young, most owners would be very happy—they wouldn't dream of separating their spawners because of their genetic makeup.

Nor would such a step be necessary if the fish are spawned simply as an outgrowth of the hobby. Yet even in such undemanding cases we owe it to ourselves to learn something about heredity so that we can understand the results of our efforts.

When breeding domestic pets and working animals, man uses his knowledge of the rules of heredity to genetically establish certain features. Farmyard pigs became longer and leaner, having been bred with more ribs to obtain more chops. Japanese breeders have spent years breeding virtually boneless carp for the table. Discus breeders, too, can influence their fish by paying attention to the rules of heredity.

Inherited features are stored in the chromosomes and genes of the parents. Some of the characteristics are dominant in the sense that they will be visible even if only one parent in a pair possesses the gene for that characteristic; others are recessive in the sense that the characteristic will show only if both parents possess the gene for it. A fish, then, can possess the gene or combination of genes for producing a particular trait and thereby have the potential for passing the trait on to its own progeny even if it does not itself show the trait. Among Discus, for example, the strong turquoise coloring that breeders strive for is a recessive trait.

The dominant features thus "prevail" over the recessive features, although the recessive features nevertheless remain stored in the genes. In general, it works out that the characteritics exhibited by wild-caught fishes are dominant and the more desirable (to us, anyway) color and shape characteristics are recessive. There are exceptions to this general rule, of course.

To bring Mendel's laws of heredity down to a common denominator, Turquoise Discus paired with a wild-caught Green Discus will produce offspring possessing in their genes the features of both, though (assuming that the wild-caught parent does not carry the gene for turquoise) only the coloration of the "normal" wild form will be visible.

Since, however, the young possess the inherited features of both, their progeny will consist of 50% mixed breeds, 25% purebred Turquoise and 25% purebred Green Discus. Of the "grandchildren" of our first breeding pair, 25% now show (and are genetically "pure" for) the pure Turquoise features; the remaining 75% look like the initial green wild-caught specimens. This color feature can now be established with the pure Turquoise Discus by inbreeding. Of course,

Just as the eggs hatched, the Discus parents moved the wriggling masses of fry from the spawning cone upon which they deposited their eggs to an aquatic plant.

water quality and the behavior and comfort of the fish also play roles as far as the color is concerned, but this does not affect the heredity. It is similarly impossible for fish whose color is a result of their having been fed with a particular color food to pass on that color in any way. Deformations, scars from injuries, and damage to the eyes through mishaps in transit are not, of course, inherited either. Even stunted growth in particular specimens is not pre-programmed in the inherited traits. Errors resulting from keeping will not affect heredity. Aquarist literature includes numerous scientific works on heredity, most of which are difficult to understand and don't make for very easy reading. An exception is the book *Genetics for the Aquarist*, published by T.F.H.

Publications, Inc. and available at pet shops everywhere.

Many Discus breeders who have been line-breeding or inbreeding with their stock of Discus for a period of time have problems with their fish, especially as regards a reduction in size.

In line-breeding, Discus of related lines are paired. Line-breeding often allows the preservation and continuance of the best features of different lines.

Inbreeding presents certain risks. If fish from two different inbred strains are crossed after at least seven generations of inbreeding, large and sensational Discus progeny may result. The problem is that these fish, unfortunately, won't pass their good features on to their young. The quality of the young

Notice the fine little
"bubbles" which are
eaten by the fry.

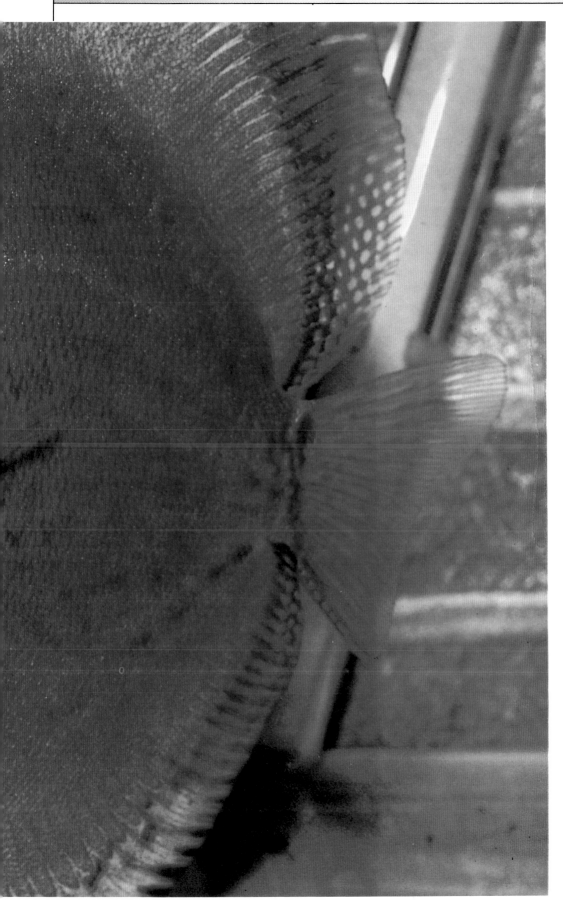

These eggs are about to die. Notice the very fine film of bacteria which appears as a cast on the surface of the eggs. First the egg goes off-color, then the bacteria invade the egg, kill it, and fungi attack as a secondary infection. The eggs must be killed before the fungus can attack. This beautiful Cobalt Discus is trying in vain to save her spawn.

Tank-raised hybrid Discus resulting from crossing a Heckel and a Royal Blue, which means crossing *Symphysodon discus* with *Symphysodon aequifasciata.* This photo was taken by available light and hardly shows true color; it is meant to show color pattern.

will be much less than that of their parents; the young will be seen to have deteriorated substantially. Another result of the crossing of distantly related inbred lines occasionally is the phenomenon known as hybrid vigor. Technically known as heterosis, hyrid vigor is typified by Discus that have good size but not good looks. They can be very large, but they're far from colorful and nicely shaped.

To establish certain attractive features when breeding we must start with two related strains whose crosses produce very good results. The offspring of these crossed pairs may then be inbred with particular

success over several generations. In practice, this means that Discus A of the first strain is paired with Discus B of the second strain. The offspring resulting from this AB pairing may then be inbred to each other. Inbreeding of this kind produces solid, satisfactory results. If the Discus breeder follows these rules he will have a fine, strong Discus strain in his tanks for many years to come. The fish will look very much alike and there will be no difficulty in selling them. Breeding like this produces very pure strains of extremely similar fish. The serious breeder will then have reached his goal.

FILTRATION AND LIGHTING

Tropical fish hobbyists have a wide selection of good equipment to choose from. The selection is so large, in fact, that it is easy for each hobbyist/breeder to customize the equipment used in each tank to fit the purpose of the tank.

Every serious Discus breeder will want to design his installation according to his own requirements. There is no reason to make every Discus installation an image of all other Discus installations. Beyond considerations that are basic to the good health of the fish—proper temperature, good water quality and things like that—you can pretty much suit your own tastes.

Special tanks must be set up for breeding pairs. How large they should be is a question of personal attitude and of space. Jack Wattley, for example, breeds his Discus in an aquarium containing less than 25 gallons (100 liters) of water. Often favored are square aquaria 20 inches (50 cm) across, 20 inches (50 cm) tall and 20 inches (50 cm) deep. This provides a maximum of 30 gallons (125 litres) of water for each pair. A tank of this size could be regarded as normal, though they may be 24, 28, or 32 inches (60, 70 or 80 cm) wide. Larger tanks are more complicated to maintain, and it is also more difficult to feed fry in over-large tanks. The more water in a breeding tank, also, the easier it is for the brine shrimp nauplii used in their feeding to distribute themselves, with the result that the young do not eat all the nauplii, leaving them to die and pollute the water.

Another argument against overly large breeding tanks is the higher energy requirement. As Discus are territorial spawners—that is, they delimit a specified territory for spawning— tanks containing 30 gallons (125 liters) are entirely adequate.

Discus breeding tanks should not be placed too close to the floor. Shelves 32 to 40 inches (80 to 100 cm) above the floor are ideal on which to place the breeding tanks.

As several breeding tanks are usually placed close together, the individual tanks should be screened off from each other. Poster board or similar substance will serve well. However, there must be enough space between the tanks for the screen to be removed when necessary. Discus need rest when they spawn. The screen should be situated so that the fish from the neighboring tank cannot be seen. If the tanks are not screened, attempted scuffles might occur, the consequence being that breeding males may be diverted too often and not do a good enough job of fertilizing the eggs. If that happens, much of the clutch would fungus. Sometimes, though, removing the screen provides beneficial results.

Some Discus pairs tend to eat their own eggs, but once the brooding fish see another Discus in the adjoining tank, their drive to protect their own eggs appears to be strengthened and they no longer attempt to eat them.

Other Discus pairs may quarrel

Young Discus feel very comfortable in a well-planted community aquarium provided there are no aggressive fishes in the same tank. They eat and grow well and can be kept there until they begin to pair off and show an interest in spawning.

fiercely after the eggs have been laid. Each wishes to guard the "nest." Time and again, therefore, the pairs have to be separated, just one parent being left to look after the brood. Here, too, visible neighboring fish may ensure that the parents do not fight, as they have then of course to deal first with the rivals in the adjoining aquarium. Many experiments can therefore be successfully concluded through manipulation of screens between the tanks.

Each breeding tank should be operated as a self-contained unit. If every tank has its own filter there is less risk of the transfer of diseases from tank to tank. If a centralized filtration system is used, diseases can affect every tank instead of being restricted to only one. With the use of a centralized system, it is even possible that eggs in one tank may be adversely affected when water is changed in an adjoining tank. Foam plastic cartridge filters are ideal for the breeding tank; sponge filters are good also. No fry or larvae can be drawn into such filters. However, when the small Discus have grown a little and are no longer so dependent on their parents, enough space should be left between the filter and the aquarium wall to allow the young to pass between them without becoming jammed.

These simple filter systems suffice with regular water changing. They are operated by air, so their use requires a good air pump. Don't stint on the purchase of such a pump; get a powerful one right from the beginning of your

The author, Bernd Degen, keeps and breeds thousands of Discus every year. His "secret," if there is such a thing, is to tame the Discus until they feed from his hands. It is only at this time that he even considers breeding or selling them. The fish shown here is called a *Brilliant Turquoise*.

breeding activities, because chances are that you'll be setting up more and more filters as you achieve success.

There are a great many filtration methods that are suitable for keeping Discus. Large external filters have proved worthwhile. Many hobbyists have linked whole batteries of Discus tanks in their basements to one large external filter. The filter chambers for installations of this kind are run with rotary pumps that are suspended directly in the clear water chamber in the filter. From here, the water is pumped into a ring delivery pipe, the water being supplied to each tank through a special valve. The foul water is conveyed to the filter from the tank through a long overflow pipe. Keep in mind that a system like this has

the potential for a disastrous transference of disease organisms and parasites from tank to tank.

Larger individual tanks intended for raising young fish or for keeping several large specimens can be run with fast-acting internal filters, but I prefer external filters. Fast rotary pumps pump the purified water from the clear water chamber directly to the tank. Foul water is removed from the tank through a simple overflow pipe and taken to the filter. Small external filters should have a large filter chamber and a smaller clear water chamber. The filter chamber may contain filter wadding, aquarium gravel, nitrate anion exchanger resin, and two layers of plastic foam in sequence from bottom to top. Filter chambers of this kind can be run for several months without any problem. The exchanger resins can be re-used after regeneration and the wadding and gravel immediately after washing out. The foam plastic mats are used for coarse filtration and are rinsed out weekly. A good rule of thumb for the minimum size of a filter such as described here is to use a filter having a capacity one tenth that of the volume of the tank.

The type of filtration system you use will of course depend to some extent on your personal choice, based on your own experiences and the degree of success (or lack of it) you've had with various setups. If you don't have enough experience to make what you'd consider to be an informed judgment, check with your aquarium dealer for good advice.

As there are no water plants to clean and help to stabilize the water in a Discus installation, the aquarist must pay particular attention to water quality. For a Discus breeding installation this necessarily includes having a good conductivity meter and a pH measurement gauge. The pH value in particular must be checked regularly, because very soft aquarium water is very unstable and may quickly lose balance. Soft water tends to rise into the alkaline areas of 7.5 to 8.0 pH. Strong water movement through the filter or diffuser will release much of the captive carbon dioxide, and this will escape from the water. Quick changes in the pH of the water should be avoided, especially in the spawning tanks.

As soft water and high water temperatures are two factors which negatively influence the quality of the water, adopting a control medium can be worthwhile. Two possibilities are ozone and ultraviolet radiation.

Ultraviolet radiation tubes can be linked straight into the filter system. An average ultraviolet tube has a working life of some 7500 hours of continous operation. This means that the tubes must be replaced after 300 days at the latest, as their output is then no longer adequate. The task of the ultraviolet light is to kill germs in the water as they pass across the beams of light.

Ozone, too, has a germicidal effect. No medications may be used during ozonization.

In addition, ozone attacks the nutrient mucus on the fish's skin. Ozone should therefore be applied only until the parent Discus begin to secrete the mucus for their young. This means that the ozone system must be switched off by no later than the second day after the eggs have been laid.

Also important for healthy Discus are partial water changes. As Discus are bred and also generally kept in tanks without substrate, the bottom of the tank must be regularly cleaned. Discus produce large quantities of excrement as they are, of course, large fish. It is therefore advisable simply to vacuum off a full bucket of tank water with the excrement every day or two. One advantage is that the excrement is thereby removed; secondly, a supply of fresh water is assured. It is

Two weeks old and still tied to their mother's apron strings! This pair raised spawn after spawn without disturbing either the eggs or the fry. The only time they leave their parents' sides is when they search for food.

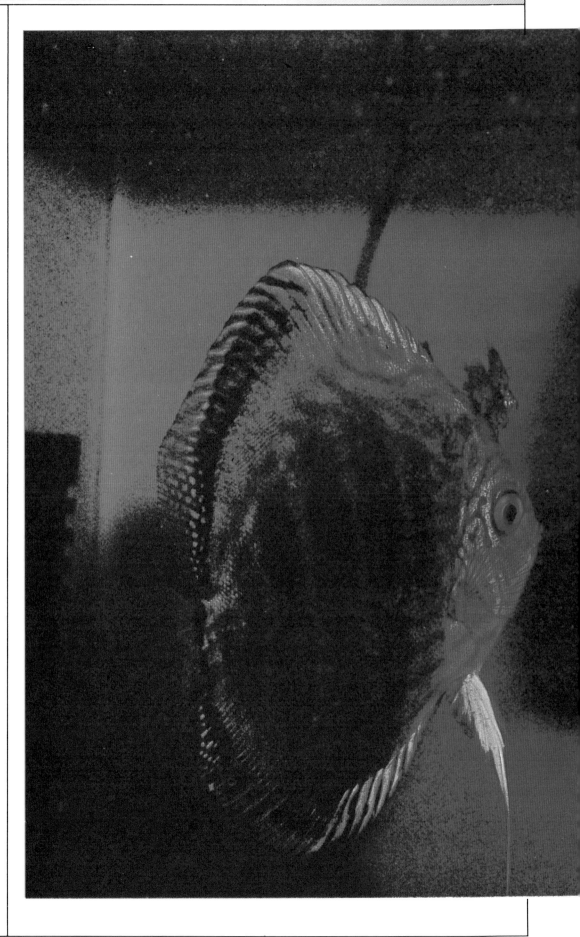

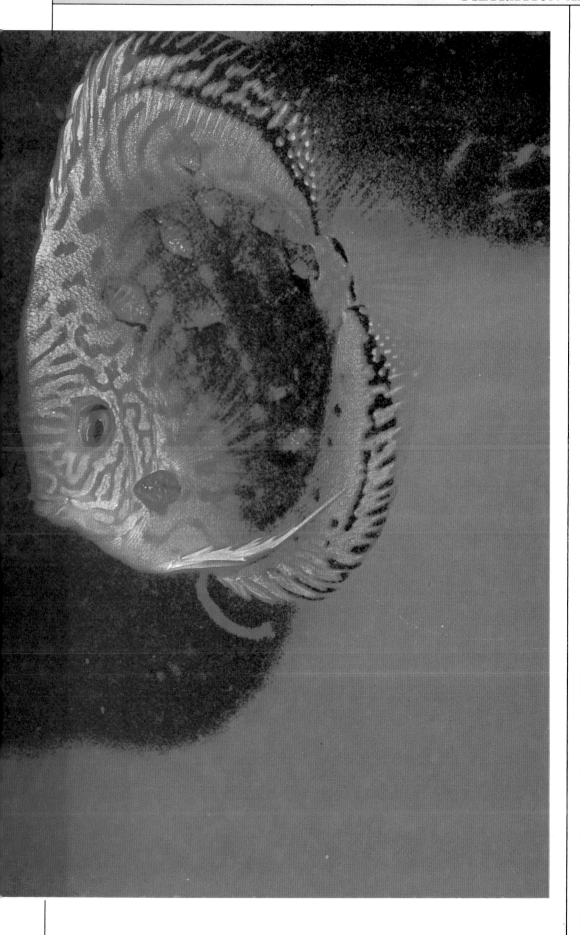

This photo was taken in available light, without a flash, in order not to disturb the parents. The baby Discus are several weeks old and could easily have been weaned to *Artemia salina*, the brine shrimp. But the beauty of watching Discus parents raising their own young and feeding them from their own body slime is almost worth the loss of spawn after spawn until the parents become dependable and stop eating the eggs or the fry.

These two photos show a tank-raised Brown Discus, *Symphysodon aequifasciata axelrodi*, above and a Green Discus hybrid of *Symphysodon a. aequifasciata* below.

beneficial to treat the new water to remove noxious chemicals such as chlorine.

A quality heater and quality thermometer are absolutely necessary for any Discus aquarium. Your dealer can recommend the brand, but you should make sure it is the best.

Of course, Discus tanks must also be lighted. Mercury vapor lamps and metal halide spots are now available for fish-keeping in addition to the traditional fluorescents, but in my opinion only the fluorescents are suitable for use on Discus tanks and breeding installations. The light intensity need not be inordinately high, especially where no plants are used. As a rule, one fluorescent light above each tank suffices. The type of bulb (warm white, cool, white, etc.) used depends mostly on individual taste. The neon tube is suspended some 8 to 12 inches (20 to 30 cm) above the water level so that it does not get in the way of work on the tank. The light yield can be increased by inserting an internal reflector to the fitting.

MAINTAINING WATER QUALITY

Keepers of Discus have to pay more attention to water quality than most other freshwater aquarists.

First of all, the pH value of the water—that is, the relative acidity or alkalinity of the water—must be regularly checked, as soft water is very unstable. The pH value scale ranges from pH 0.0 to pH 14.0, with the lower values (those below pH 7.0, which is neutral) being acidic and the higher values alkaline. Discus feel happiest in water with a pH value of between 6.0 and 7.0. For breeding purposes, the pH value should be closer to values around 6.0, as a reasonable level of acidity has a tendency to help prevent fungus from attacking the eggs. Pet shops and tropical fish specialty stores stock the measurement devices and pH-altering chemicals that might be required.

As the pH value is important to the appetite and contentment of the fish and in persuading them to reproduce, it must be regularly checked.

If you get into keeping and breeding Discus on a serious level, the purchase of an electrical pH meter could be a worthwhile investment for you. The electrode on this appliance is dipped into the aquarium water. The electrode produces an electrical voltage which is displayed on the appliance through an amplifier. Precise measurements are possible within seconds.

Another important measurement is the water's electrical conductivity. All water contains dissolved substances, salts in particular. These salt ions conduct the current. The higher the ion concentration in the water, the more conductive it becomes. The conductance of sea water, which is very rich in dissolved salts, is very high. On the other hand, the conductance of the home waters of the Discus is very low. It is generally less than 50 microsiemens. This indicates a water hardness of approximately 1 degree of general hardness, meaning that there is virtually no carbonate hardness in the water.

These factors must logically be taken into account when breeding as well. The breeding water must be made right for Discus. In many cases this requires the de-salting of the water. The osmotic pressure on the Discus egg can be reduced in this way. Under high osmotic pressure, the Discus eggs will be destroyed and eventually fungus. The destruction is generally invisible to the human eye.

The eggs remain clear for a while, but no fry develop; the internal pressure of the egg prevents their normal development.

The aquarist is happy because he can see clear eggs, but days pass without their developing further.

The conductance of the breeding water should in no event be less than 300 microsiemens, the carbonate hardness comprising the lesser part of the water hardness. The tap water in Germany, for example, is often very hard and

unsuitable for breeding. lt must therefore be softened. Industrially produced ion-exchange resins are available for this purpose. These are microscopic granules of artificial resin and have long been used in industrial water treatment.

Water softening is particularly important for Discus breeders, as hard tap water can be treated to suit the fish. Cation exchangers remove the existing carbonate. Calcium and magnesium are taken out of the water and replaced with sodium. The softening filters work very slowly. Special desalination filter columns are commercially available. They can be either integrated directly into the filter system or used as a bypass. Under the bypass system, a proportion of the filter water is passed across the resin through a hose system. The treated water is then returned to the filter chamber.

Softening resins are easily and safely regenerated with kitchen salt. Precise instructions for resins are delivered with the equipment. The sodium hydrocarbide produced by the carbonate hardness unfortunately renders the water alkaline. The pH value will fluctuate between pH 8.0 and 9.0. These values are of course undesirable for Discus. The water must therefore again be buffered with acids into safer pH areas.

The pH value must also be carefully controlled by a softening process that causes only the carbonate hardness to be removed. The carbonate hardness can be eliminated outside the aquarium by the filtration process relatively easily. The resin is regenerated with diluted hydrochloric acid. Necessary caution is of course required here, especially as regards the rinsing of the resins after regeneration. Careless use can all too easily produce a pH collapse in the tank, and the fish will die. You must not tinker with the composition of your water through the use of chemicals and associated products unless you have sufficient grounding in chemistry to understand what you're doing.

A further possibility is to desalinate the water. Something close to distilled water can be produced by a twin filter process or a mixing bed outside the aquarium. The twin filter process is simpler to operate and less complex. In the first filter water passes through a cation exchanger regenerated with acids. In the second filter it passes through an anion exchanger. The water obtained in this way must be adjusted with other desalinated water or tap water. Fully desalinated water would be tantamount to distilled water. Many aquarists have to desalinate their tap water. They then have a salt-deficient water, the important salts also unfortunately being removed by this process. Concentrations of the minerals and vitamins obtainable through the trade must then be added. Organic materials from aquarium peat must then also be applied. Only then will the water be "alive," but without the harmful salts. This desalinated and retreated water must of course be checked for the right pH value and, if necessary, adjusted upward or downward.

On the facing page is a truly magnificent prize-winning male turquoise-colored Discus. The intensity of the red and the uniform facial markings, accentuated by the large red eye, make this an extremely suitable sire.

The methods described so far for treating water are all external ones. There are also internal methods of water treatment for maintaining water quality in the tank.

An ion exchanger resin conditioned with the proper chemicals will ensure that the pH value is maintained. The carbonate hardness is kept very low, and the pH value will settle down at between pH 5.7 and 7.0.

It is, on the other hand, very important for the Discus keeper that metabolic products are removed together with the nitrates.

As our installations will not include aquatic nitrate-consuming plants in any quantity, the harmful nitrates must again be eliminated by more frequent partial water changing or nitrate filtration. An anion exchanger in chloride form which can be installed like filter charcoal has proved useful for this purpose. This means that the resin is used as a post-filtration material in the external filter or a canister filter. Wadding, gravel, or a similar material is used for pre-filtration. One liter of exchanger resin should be used for every 20 gallons (80 litres) of tank volume, so that— assuming a normal complement of fish— a working life is achieved for the filter of three to six months. The resin is then reactivated with kitchen salt solution. A very simple and safe method.

This is a wild *Symphysodon aequifasciata aequifasciata* Discus which comes from the Rio Purus in Brazil. The Japanese call this a *Peruvian Green*, but it is not from Peru.

Compare the
profiles of the
Discus on this and
the facing page.
Note the pug-face
of the fish shown
below compared to
the almost modest
features of the fish
to the left.

The anion exchanger binds hydrogen to carbonate and so also slightly reduces the carbonate hardness. In addition, the pH value is buffered in the pH 5.7 to 7.0 range, which is ideal for Discus.

With this resin, the nitrate content is kept practically at zero for months at a time. This especially favors the growth of the young.

As the valuable humic acids, e. g. from aquarium peat, should be retained in the Discus tank, care must be taken when using this resin that the type purchased will allow the humic acids to be retained in the water. A version is in fact commercially available that removes the humic acids without trace; it is of no use for Discuskeeping.

The application of these exchange resins makes both the keeping and breeding of Discus much easier. There is the proviso, however, that the keeper should be fully familiar with the systems.

It is particularly important that nitrates should be removed from water in which Discus are bred, successful breeders swearing by a maximum nitrate value of 0. 15 mg per liter of water.

GETTING READY

It goes without saying that you can't breed Discus unless you have a male and a female. Some Discus fanciers have the time to compose their pairs from fish that they've raised themselves, but others must buy adult fish before they start their Discus breeding operations.

It is a fact that there are no sure external characteristics for determining the sex, and one can only go by assumptions. However, in the course of time the breeder will gain a sixth sense, both in sexing his fish and also when buying the fish he needs from other breeders.

What characteristics can we use to determine the sex? First of all, there is the general appearance of the fish. With fish of the same age, the males are generally more thickset and rather larger. Especially when viewed from the front, the males have broader and outwardly more strongly rounded skulls. The dorsal fins of male specimens generally come to a longer point and tend to curve upwards. Females have rather more rounded ends to their dorsal fins. Additionally, the caudal fin of the male Discus may appear rather broader than that of the female.

The ventral fins may also be longer and broader in the male, though this characteristic should be evaluated with caution.

Powerful skulls, thick lips and a marked "dewlap" are commonly ascribed to males, though large females may also, of course, display these features.

Behavior in the tank also can be an indication, but keep in mind that the leader of a group of Discus may be either a male or a female. Generally speaking, when two fish are kept together in a tank the male will set the pace. A pair will not normally tug at each other's mouths. The male will lightly dig the female in the side. He swims rapidly toward her, then suddenly turns away. The female usually displays her dark stripes clearly. If the fish are compatible and if the presumed male allows his partner to feed with him untroubled, they are certainly a pair. If, on the other hand, one of the fish hides in a corner of the aquarium when food is given, the two fish will be of the same sex.

Well proved is the method of placing two fish which form a presumed pair in a tank. After a few days there can be little further doubt as to the sexes. If the two quarrel heavily they must be separated. When forming a new pair, the males should always be placed with the female already in the tank. The transferred male must then first get his bearings and cannot immediately dash at the physically inferior female. If, on the other hand, a Discus female is put into a tank in which a male is already established, she will soon be violently embraced and spend several days hiding in corners and at the water surface.

The female of this pair is in the foreground. She is smaller than the male and has less intense coloration. However, her genetic makeup is such that non-apparent (genotypic) characteristics enable her to produce outstanding offspring when mated to an outstanding male.

It is absolutely necessary that a pair be socially compatible before their sexual compatibility is considered. The successful Discus breeder should observe the fish to see if they look and act peacefully, especially during feeding time.

The two photos above show the same color fish, but how they photograph depends upon the available light reflection. In the lower photo we see a typical German Discus hatchery.

PREPARING THE TANK

Unfortunately, only a few fry were left after the mother Discus went on a rampage and ate them. These few are 4 days old and are beginning to eat newly hatched brine shrimp, *Artemia salina*. Once they eat *Artemia* they can be isolated from their parents.

Apart from optimum breeding specimens, the technical facilities and the water quality must also be adjusted to breeding. The water should not only be prepared as mentioned but enriched with peat extract. For this purpose, aquarium peat can be mixed with water in a separate tank or in a plastic container. Aerated by means of an air stone, the peat will then add humic acids to the water. A proportion of this old water can be conveyed to the breeding tank after a few days. The fish will generally react positively to the slight change in the pH value and to the new composition of the water and possibly be stimulated to spawn. This is precisely the phenomenon that occurs in nature when new water is added during the rainy season. The peat can be bundled in gauze bags or a nylon stocking so it does not spread in the container. Another possibility would be to turn off the aeration system for a few hours so that the peat sludge can settle on the bottom of the container.

Ceramic vases have proved ideal as a spawning substrate for the eggs, but Discus will of course also spawn on other articles. The spawning substrate should not have too smooth a surface, which is why ceramic pots have proved very useful. Even ordinary clay flowerpots can be used, but the hole in the pot should be closed up; if it is not, the fry may otherwise swim into it. In addition, sludge suspended in the

If you are going to breed Discusfish, make up your mind as to your breeding objectives, then get the best specimens available. Don't waste your time breeding substandard Discus. It takes just as much time and effort to breed valuable Discus.

water may also collect in it.

The right location for the breeding tank is also a criterion for the breeder to consider. Discus like to spawn in peace unless they have been completely accustomed to the hustle and bustle of human activity around them. Discus breeding facilities are often set up in basement rooms where the fish are unlikely to be disturbed, especially if the keeper enters the room only occasionally. The fish panic and attempt to flee on a sudden disturbance or too much movement in the room. It has been proved that fish will become used to noise, disturbance and movement in front of the tank. The more disturbance regularly occurs, the less timid the fish will be. On bathing beaches with many bathers in the water, fish swim quite happily among the bathers without thinking of flight. Animals in zoos or wildlife parks are not frightened of people, as they are used to seeing them. The situation is the same with Discus.

If they are healthy, Discus will swim to the glass out of curiosity when a visitor stands in front of the aquarium. In fact, they should even be willing to take food from the hand. Discus get used to people and know precisely when it is feeding time and will then swim up toward them. This is another of the joys of keeping Discus.

The female Discus lays her eggs on the leaf of an Amazon Swordplant. The male anxiously awaits his turn to fertilize the newly laid eggs.

THE ACTUAL SPAWNING

Whether they admit it or not, most freshwater aquarium hobbyists want to breed Discus. It's certainly a worthwhile goal, especially if the principles set out in this book are observed when selecting the breeding pair. Being able to observe the interesting brood care of the Discus, which long remained unknown, is adequate compensation for a great deal of trouble. Does the hobby have anything finer to offer than the self-sacrificing brood care of two compatible parent fish? They look after the eggs and fan them tirelessly, subsequently releasing the fry lovingly from the eggs and re-bedding them. When the fry swim freely, they make sure that none is lost. Time and again they swim off after the small fry to bring them back to the fold. When, eventually, the fry swim freely, the parent fish offer them their skin secretion and unflinchingly allow themselves to be grazed upon by a host of tiny mouths. The parent fish care for their young like this for weeks on end, until the young have become independent. These weeks are probably the finest for the owner, who will continuously rush to his aquarium to see his splendid brood.

But the fish must first spawn before that point is reached. When a Discus pair have "found" each other, they are bound to spawn soon. The process may greatly try their owner's patience. It may take weeks or even months until so-called "compatible" fish spawn. They are already sexually mature when barely one year old. Discus will spawn really effectively while they are between one and three years of age.

It is said of Discus that they start to spawn during periods of low atmospheric pressure. However, this hypothesis is not the only one in circulation. The females can produce a clutch of eggs every week for many weeks during a spawning phase. One Discus female can deposit up to 20 clutches in this way within six months.

Normally, of course, the female will look after her brood and then spawn again only when the fry are taken from the tank. However, this repeated egg-laying has been observed of notorious eggeaters. Between the spawning phases the fish may have rest periods of several months. It may happen, therefore, that good pairs will suddenly make no further attempts to spawn for months, and then as suddenly start up again.

The first hint the Discus give of their impending reproductive activities is a change in their colors.

The rear part of the body, in particular, turns darker. The last four stripes become visible, and the tail fin looks sooty. The fish also begin to darken all along their bodies, which indicates that spawning is imminent.

The fish stand peacefully at the spawning cone. Now and then a shiver passes through their bodies. This is particulary noticeable at the head end. The fish's fins quiver and they swim toward each other. A

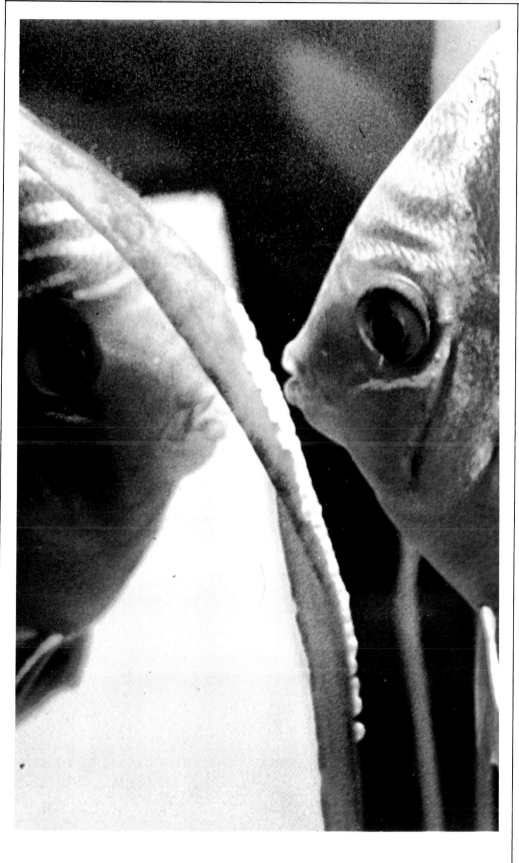

The parents care for the eggs by fanning them and blowing water at them to remove debris and bring freshly oxygenated water to the developing eggs.

The spawning was in vain! As soon as the eggs were laid, the parents began to eat them! They usually spawn once again a week later.

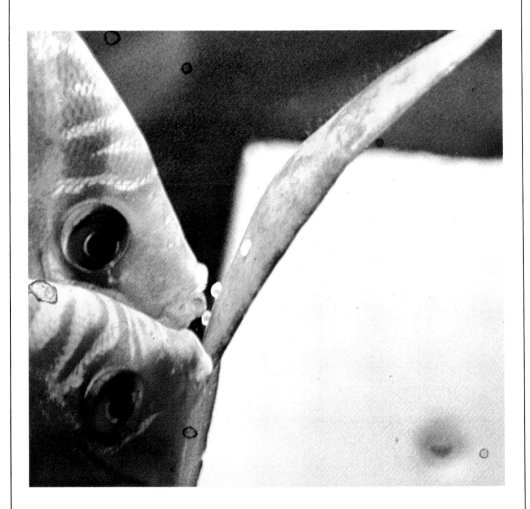

nodding motion can also be observed.

The female now swims repeatedly to the ceramic cone and appears to spawn. However, she is not yet ready. Again and again, both partners clean the spawning substrate. The fish suck dirt off the cone, scrubbing it hard. This cleaning process is a sure sign that spawning is imminent.

The female's ovipositor now becomes visible. This broad tube projects 3 to 4 millimeters from the body. The male's generative organ is shorter and comes to a point.

The female repeatedly starts test-spawning, but at this stage the male is just an interested bystander. That is why other aquariums should be masked off, so the fish are not diverted.

After the preparations for spawning, which may take a whole day, actual spawning commences.

Discus spawn preferably during the evening. The female starts out low on the spawning cone and lays one egg after the other on her way up. She will untiringly deposit an average of ten to twenty eggs in rows. The average clutch contains 200 eggs; good clutches contain some 300 eggs and top clutches 400 to 500. After every successive egg deposit the female makes room for the male so that he can immediately fertilize the eggs. There should at this point be no rapid current in the breeding tank. The filter must be throttled down.

A spawning session takes about one hour. The fish can be observed, but they must not be disturbed. The sex can now be determined with absolute certainty, and now and again a presumed female may prove to be male. It is also important to see whether the fish tolerate each other well. The better a Discus pair gets along, the greater the chances of survival for the fry. If the young fish can consistently choose between the skin secretion of both parents, their stomachs will always be full and they will grow faster in the first days.

After the eggs have been laid, the parents position themselves in front of the clutch and fan the eggs with their pectorals. Harmonious pairs will relieve each other at regular intervals. If the parents begin to squabble, the situation may become critical. If the squabbles get worse, the parents will probably eat the eggs as a result. Removing one of the fish may not even help, because the fish left behind will promptly make for the eggs. However, even single fish can successfully raise young.

It repeatedly happens that Discus eat the fry after the eggs have hatched. A solution in this case, too, can be to remove one fish from the breeding tank. A wet-nurse is even a possibility if the conditions are right. If, for example, another Discus pair has young at much the same time, the fry can be removed from the tank with quarrelsome parents and slipped into the school of other young. The new parents will not usually notice and will readily accept the additional fry. The eggs can also be taken from egg-eating parents in the same way and left to hatch artificially, and the fry then can be smuggled in with

This male parent is vainly attempting to keep his school of fry together. They have just hatched and have not started to eat from the parents' bodies yet. This is a very critical time for the fry, as the parents might eat them as a result of the turmoil.

another brooding pair. Valuable young of poor parents can thus be raised naturally.

However, let's get back to the egg-laying in the breeding tank. The eggs need some 60 hours at a temperature of 86 F. (30 C.) to develop. By the second day, dark spots inside the eggs will have become visible to the naked eye. After 48 hours small eyes can even be seen.

The attentive parents help as soon as the fry begin to hatch from the eggs. They simply chew the fry out of the eggs. The fry adhere to the spawning substrate and jerkily vibrate their tails.

Adhesive glands in the head prevent them from falling off. This stage ends after a further 60 hours, when the fry begin to swim free. The parents will often re-bed the young at this stage. The fry are settled at a different spot from the one to which the eggs adhered. Many a Discus-lover has sought his young charges in vain the next day, only suddenly to rediscover them later. The parents had simply re-bedded them.

During this stage of development, from egg to free-swimming small Discus, a nightlight should be left burning near the tank so the parents have time to gather up the fry in the evening and look after them overnight.

During this time the parents eat less but should still be fed regularly. Live food should be avoided, though, as this confuses the fish, forcing them to distinguish between the young and the live food, which they find difficult to do.

This Discus female is in the actual process of depositing eggs. Her pointed ovipositor is shown extended. The male is seen closely standing by awaiting his task of fertilizing the eggs. The ovipositor is sensitive to touch. The eggs are laid close to one another, but none is laid atop another egg.

During the first week or so, the fry are almost totally dependent upon their parents for slime food. Sometimes after 3-4 days they will take a few freshly hatched brine shrimp. These photos show fry up to 2 days old, at which age they certainly must be kept with their parents unless you know how to feed them powdered egg food.

It is important that the young should swim toward the parent fish as soon as they swim free. If they do not do so, they are lost. This happens quite often, and the reason for it is not known. It is also possible that the parents fail to develop the skin secretion, in which case the brood is similarly lost. The young that swim to the parents remain almost constantly in contact with their skin and eat the secretion almost uninterruptedly. At this period the parents also adopt a particularly dark color.

For the first few days, the young will feed exclusively off the parents' skin secretion. Without the secretion, survival is not possible by natural means. Some breeders have tried, with a great deal of trouble and greater or lesser success, to raise Discus artificially. Whether artificial raising is to be aimed at need not concern us here. Were it to become the rule, it would soon mean an end to the Discus, as the Discus would then have to follow the same road as the Angelfish. It would then be bred only for financial gain, and young specimens would flood the market. Breeders looking for quality would breed smaller numbers, if any at all. The result would be a collapse of quality standards.

The skin secretion is vital to the young for at least the first four or five days, as they will eat no other food. Only then can the breeder start topping up their food with brine shrimp.

While the young will initially always stay with the parents, they make for the baby brine shrimp as

Taken in almost total darkness so as not to upset this Discus mother, this photo shows the lone parent raising a fairly substantial brood. The male was so aggressive that he had to be removed to save the brood and the female. The female successfully raised all the fry by herself!

Discus eggs take 60 hours to become free-swimming fry. At 48 hours they are still stuck to the breeding cone. After hatching, the fry fall to the bottom, where they congregate until they discover their parents. They start feeding immediately as they have already used up their yolk.

soon as it is fed. In these first days they will venture as much as 2 inches (5 centimeters) away from the parents. As they grow older, the bond between fry and parents weakens.

It is interesting to note how the parents change roles while feeding the brood. Generally, one fish swims with the young while the other keeps an eye open for food in the tank or guards the territory.

A Discus pair will raise young even in the presence of other large specimens. The other inmates will keep well clear of a couple with young. The pair and their young will take over at least half of the aquarium.

The small fish will feed off the parents' secretion for two weeks in total. The period may be extended by a day or two, but by then the young will have reached such a size that they may damage the parents' mucous membranes. The time has then come to separate the fry from the parents.

After the fry have eaten their first *Artemia* nauplii they will increasingly go for this food. To start with, the breeder will blow the nauplii directly into the school of young near the parents with a glass pipette. Later on, the small Discus will search all over the tank for the shrimp. Within two weeks the baby fish will also greedily take fine flake and other prepared foods that have been pulverized or otherwise treated so as to reduce them to a size ingestible by the fry.

This is a head study of a magnificently colored Green Turquoise Discus. The red eye is a desirable objective for inbreeding, as is the sturdy head structure.

Feeding from the parent is common to all Discusfishes, even though in many of South America's river systems it is not necessary for the fish to be parasitic on their parents. The baby Discus usually feed on one parent at a time. When that parent is ready to change, it signals its mate and the mate approaches, enabling the fry to swim over for another meal.

The male, the lighter of the two fish, is passing the young to the female. It is the dream of every Discus breeder to have a breeding pair of Discus that will raise their young in a planted home aquarium.

CARE OF THE FRY

Getting a pair of Discus to spawn is only part of the battle; raising them can be even more difficult.

Once he has succeeded in breeding Discus, every breeder is faced with the problem of raising the young successfully. Raising in some cases can mean that he keeps the fish for six to eight weeks and then sells them. However, it can also mean keeping them until they reach adulthood, which entails caring for them for nine to twelve months.

As small Discus are generally sold at the age of eight weeks or so, it is important for them to be kept healthy during this period. To do so, the making of partial water changes on a regular basis is important.

One way to avoid the risk of a rise in the water's nitrate content is to fit a nitrate filter to the raising tank. Discus young kept in excessive nitrate will show poor growth.

As these fish need feeding several times a day, their metabolic output is correspondingly high. The water is burdened with an above-average quantity of waste products. That is why the partial daily water change, with the impurities being vacuumed oif, is so important. As fish generally grow better in harder, i. e., mineral-rich, water, tap water can safely be used for raising the young. Up to 20 degrees of general hardness are acceptable in this case. The harder water is also far more stable as regards pH value. The risk of having the pH value suddenly falling or rising sharply is then more remote.

Attention must remain focused on good water quality at all times. If fed well and adequately, the young fish will then grow rapidly. The fry will already have reached a size of about 1.25 inches (3 centimeters) after six weeks.

Damage to the gill covers is a recurring problem with young Discus. There is still no hard and fast explanation as to what causes such damage, although two theories have been advanced. The first is that in an overly small aquarium and with poor water quality, the oxygen supply may be insufficient for the young fish. They then stand in the tank, panting wildly. This may distort the gill covers. If the water quality is poor, inflammation of the gills may become an additional symptom.

The second theory is a deficiency in minerals and vitamins for the young fish. This is perfectly possible, since in the first three weeks of their lives the fish generally eat only brine shrimp apart from the skin secretion. Vitamin concentrates should always be added to the brine shrimp cultures. One drop of multi-vitamin solution should be supplied for each newly started culture after 20 hours, when the brine shrimp nauplii begin to hatch. The addition of enough mineral product (enough to cover a knife-tip) might also help.

This is a beautiful solid (almost) Brilliant Turquoise Discus. It is assuming spawning color. The rough skin in back of the eye is not a disease but a common skin abnormality, much like a wart.

THE IMPORTANCE OF GOOD FEEDING

Discus are relatively large fish, by aquarium standards, and they're big eaters, too. But they're not greedy, sloppy eaters; they're dainty eaters—and they're picky as well.

Quite the opposite of the Angel, which darts quickly at any kind of food, the Discus is far more choosy. In the wild, the various Discusfishes have to live chiefly on mayflies and their larvae or on small freshwater crustaceans such as shrimps of the genus *Macrobrachium.*

To what extent Discus also eat large quantities of algae has not yet been adequately researched. Some researchers say that they do.

Given time, Discus can be acclimated to a number of the commercially prepared foods available in the aquarium hobby. A newly acquired Discus will not, of course, eat in its new owner's tank on the first day. However, when put into the company of Discus that have become accustomed to eating flake foods and other prepared foods, they'll come around fairly soon. The need for food is basic and soon ensures that all fishes eat. Discus that leave the school while being fed are undoubtedly sick.

Specifically not recommended as a food for Discus are tubifex worms. These worms are generally so contaminated and polluted with dirt and heavy metals that they should not be used for feeding. Large Discus do not generally take to freeze-dried mosquito larvae, as they float on the surface, even when they are very small. Frozen bloodworms are a different story. Another staple feed for Discus is beefheart. A heart free of sinews and fat is cut into small pieces and frozen, or ready-to-use beefheart can be purchased in frozen form from aquarium shops.

When needed, a hard piece of beefheart can be grated on a vegetable or nut grater, and appliances are also available for this purpose. If the heart is grated in the deep-frozen state, small worm-like strips will result; the fish will readily take these strips. To improve the content, the heart can be injected with vitamins or mineral preparations before being frozen. A syringe with a needle is needed for this purpose. A multi-vitamin or mineral product is placed in the syringe and injected into the meat in small doses. The meat can then be frozen. The product injected in this way is also frozen and mixed directly with the meat on thawing out. In this way, the Discus obtain enriched heart meat, an important ingredient in their diet.

Another possibility would be to cut the heart into pieces after removing the fat, and reduce it in a blender, depending on the size of the fish. To this pulp a multi-vitamin mineral product can be added. Chopped, boiled spinach, raw egg yolk, and paprika powder can be added as well. The pulp is then put into a plastic bag, with the mass distributed as a thin plate, and is frozen. Small cubes can then be easily broken off the thin plate.

If a Discus lives long enough it will develop a bump on its forehead. This is probably for storage of excess fat. If the Discus is less than 3 years old and has developed or is developing this lumpy forehead, the diet you are offering is too rich in fats.

Discus are slow and deliberate eaters that prefer to feed from the bottom. They can spend the whole day poking about the bottom looking for a morsel.

Freeze-dried mosquito larvae can also be mixed into the beefheart pulp. The larvae then absorb the moisture and descend into the tank with the heart, where they are then easily eaten.

Enchytraeid worms are another good Discus food. The hobbyist can raise the small white worms himself. These worms are taken avidly and are a good means of getting the female to spawn. However, as they are very fatty the quantities given should be kept within bounds. The worms are invaluable for young fish as well. If, in fact, white worms are fed together with highly albuminous substances, the fish will obtain important (even if not strictly essential) albumens. Vitamin powder can also be scattered on the worm cultures and the worms enriched with vitamins in this way.

Water fleas like *Daphnia*, on the other hand, are a food willingly taken only by smaller Discus. Adult Discus are too big to bother with them.

When introducing Discus to a new food form, the Discus-keeper will have to slowly acclimate his fish to the new food by feeding them small quantities daily to start with, then slowly increasing the amount. Whether a Discus will take to a new food or not is very much a matter of patience on the part of the aquarist. Quality dry food has advantages which must be given due consideration. Three to four feedings a day would be ideal for large Discus. Feed little but often is the rule— dry food in the morning or afternoon, with a portion of live or deep-frozen food in the evening. The fish should be allowed at least fifteen minutes before feeding in the morning to become really active. The Discus will eat nothing immediately after the light is switched on. They must first regain their fine hues; the color of the eye, in particular, must be clearly visible. If it is not, it means the fish are not yet active.

Young fish in principle eat the same as an adult Discus. The young should, however, be fed several times a day, the more often the better, but only in such quantities as are quickly eaten up. Members of the family staying at-home can perhaps feed them with dry food and tablets while the Discus-breeder will offer the small fish a delicacy in the early morning or at night, using more laborious means.

Unfortunately, small Discus cannot be left at home for days at a time without food. The damage would be too great. Someone must in fact be found who is prepared to feed them at least twice a day. This applies up to about their twelfth week. From then on, feeding only once a day will do for a period of time. Adult Discus can tolerate going hungry for a week, but that's no reason to let them go hungry that long. In any event, the fish should be fed more abundantly for several days before a holiday or weekend trip taken by their feeder.

Red mosquito larvae (bloodworms) are very well accepted by Discus. They are available in frozen form. Unfortunately, frozen bloodworms contain heavy metals and should be fed sparingly. Most dry fishfoods also contain heavy metals. Contact the food manufacturers or packagers and ask them about the metal content of their foods. The probable safe concentration of iron in water is 3 parts in 100 million or 0.03 p.p.m. The safe concentration for copper is about half that of iron.

DISEASE TREATMENT

Some hobbyists have the idea that if you just look at a Discus the wrong way it'll get sick. Such is not the case at all—it's just that the ailments that plague Discus have been too shrouded in a veil of secrecy. As with all other ornamental fishes, we must get to the root of the trouble with Discus as well. The supreme commandment in disease prevention is be sure of your water quality. We keep these fish in aquaria holding only several hundred liters of water while, in nature, several thousand liters flow past our Discus every minute.

Logically, the risk of the water deteriorating in a small aquarium is much greater than in nature. There is, therefore, a much greater danger of the outbreak of disease simply because the quality of the water is less good. This can be prevented, in turn, by regular partial changes of water, large filter chambers, suitable filter substrate and nitrate filtration.

Factors that produce disease among aquarium fishes are ammonia and nitrite poisoning, rapid changes in the pH value, temperature drops, lack of oxygen and intoxication through foreign substances. To this may be added unsuitable transport of the fish, transfer to a new aquatic environment, overpopulation of the tank and the introduction of disease by new fish.

The food given to the fish also plays an important part as regards susceptibility to disease. The poorer a Discus eats, the more susceptible it becomes. If the food given is too uniform, often just to suit the aquarist, the fish will not be adequately provided with the right nutrients. That is why variety is important when feeding.

Fish can also be over-fed. As fishes in captivity never have the same amount of swimming space as those swimming in freedom, their over-all metabolic rate consequently is lower. This must be also taken into account. Fishes can, in fact, overeat, and this produces serious disruption of the metabolism, fatty livers, etc.

Newly acquired fish should in any event be put into quarantine. This is particularly advisable with Discus since they are, after all, expensive fish. The newcomers can be provided with disease-preventive treatment during their quarantine, using medications recommended for prophylaxis during quarantine. The fish should remain in the quarantine bath for at least five days. This tank is filtered through wadding and run on an aerator. The temperature should be 86° F. (30° C.). If the fish are in good condition the temperature can during these five days be raised to 90° F. (32-33° C.). A good supply of oxygen must then be provided.

After this period of quarantine the new fish can be transferred to the community tank without further ado.

Many medications from human medicine are now used for Discus as well. These medications, which

The photo shows a Discus being treated by having medicine squirted into its stomach, using a nutrient solution (liquefied shrimp or worms) as a liquid vehicle.

Look closely at the craters over the eye! This indicates `hole-in-the-head disease caused by *Spironucleus*. It should be treated with *Clout* immediately. Without treatment this malady often is deadly.

Help with Discus Diseases

SYMPTOM	CAUSE	TREATMENT
Pop-eye	Bacteria Very poor water quality	Immediate partial water change. 1 table of "Cotrim Forte" (A) (an antibiotic) per 25 gallons (100 liters) of water Repeat treatment at half dosage if no improvement after two days.
Milky skin, White spots	*Costia* sp. *Ichtyobodo necatrix*	500 mg Trypaflavin and 5 mg Malachite green oxalate per 25 gallons (100 liters) of water for 3 days
Choking, Heavy breathing, Nervous swimming	Gill worms	"Flubenol 5%" 200 mg per 25 gallons (100 liters). Repeat twice at 7-day intervals after water exchange with same dosage.
Long white fecal threads	Nematodes, tapeworms	"Flubenol" (See dosage above.)
Refusal to eat, gelatinous fecal threads	Threadworms, intestinal problems	Long bath with "Masoten," 50 mg/25 gallons at 82 degrees F. (28° C.). Change ¼ of water (treated with ¼ of Masoten dosage) daily for four days. Water exchange after four days.
Poor appetite, very dark color, gelatinous feces, abnormal behavior "Hole in the head" disease (crater-like holes in head region).	Intestinal flagellates: *Hexamita,* *Protoopalina,* *Spironucleus*	Long bath in Clout (A), 1T with 250 mg Metronidazol in 50 L water or Metronidazol as pure-substance from the pharmacist. After 4 days make 50% water change and repeat the same treatment. Perhaps apply the dosage on food tablets or use syringe.
Skin disease, rubbing on tank accoutrements	Bacteria on skin	Short bath (maximum 30 minutes) of 150 mg Leukomycin in 2.5 gallons (10 liters of water). Use aquarium water.

NOTE: You must always be careful when using drugs and other chemicals in the aquarium, if for no other reason than that water quality can be different in each tank—and of course every Discus is different also. Use drugs only with great caution and exactitude.

A = Pharmacy prescription needed.

If you closely examine the lateral line you will find a few series of enlarged scales. These are common abnormalities. They cannot be treated and are of no concern as far as the fish's health goes.

are very effective, are obtainable only from a pharmacy or through a veterinarian. Many of those drugs used in human and veterinary medicine are available only on prescription, of course.

Apart from the ordinary fish diseases such as *Costia* and *Ichthyophthirius multifiliis*, for which effective medications are available through the pet trade, there are diseases specific to the Discus. Flagellates, intestinal worms, gill worms, and other parasites are a recurring nuisance with Discus. Worm infestation is common and can be detected from the white, tough excrement.

Frequent chafing against ornaments in the tank is also a cause of worry to the keeper.

All of these conditions are listed in the accompanying table.

A very effective tonic for ailing Discus is to heat up the aquarium water substantially. This may prove successful, especially with fish producing white excrement and with dark fish off their food. The aquarium water must be heated to 95 degrees F (35° C.) under careful control and with a good oxygen supply. This must be done slowly. Cool off again slowly to normal temperature after a week.

With hole-in-the-head disease, this period can be extended to two weeks. It will be obvious that heat treatment of this kind places a heavy burden on the fish, but the success is often remarkable. However, this heat treatment may be too much for a weak, very thin fish. In the case of very sick specimens that no longer eat and

that are thin and produce white excrement, syringing medication into the mouth should certainly be attempted. Perseverance is necessary.

When Discus are feeding their young via skin secretions, their color and slime covering change. This is not a disease. If the young die or are eaten by the parents or other fish, the slime coating may slough off. This is a normal condition and does not have to be treated.

123

These two Discus are suffering from an unknown skin malady. The body starts to lose color intensity, the fins become frayed and the fish die. Some Discus can successfully be treated with an antihistamine. In 1990, this was a disease restricted to Discus imported from Singapore. Antibiotics and other normal treatments of Discus diseases failed to help. Neither parasites nor bacterial diseases could be identified. This might be a traumatic condition brought on by water changes, light periodicity or food substitution.

DEGEN'S TREATMENT FOR DISCUS

Medicines from the human range are particulary important to Discus keepers. They can be used to cure Discus rapidly of serious, fatal illnesses. Discus frequently die from an infestation with flagellates or tapeworms. We have the medications Flagyl and Simplotan available in this case, which are used in human medicine to control trichomonads. The medicines are available only from a chemist. In the past, a dosage was recommended of 4 mg Flagyl per liter or 1 g of Simplotan tablet per 25 gallons (100 liters) of water. However, as absorption through water is very poor, I have devised the following methods.

First of all, take a tablet of Simplotan, or two tablets of Flagyl, or 500 mg of Metronidazol, rub them fine and mix them with six crushed food tablets. Now carefully add one drop of water to form a spreadable paste. Spread the paste over ten food tablets and leave them to dry overnight. Now administer them in the ordinary way. I have regularly given this food for preventive purposes, e. g. once a month for two days consecutively. If the fish are no longer taking food, they will of course be beyond recovery. That is why I developed a second, highly effective method, as follows: 500 mg of Metronidazol is dissolved in 2. 5 gallons (10 liters) of water. For this purpose I use an empty cough mixture bottle or something similar. I then take a plastic syringe (without needle) and suck up the dissolved medication. The fish is removed from the tank and placed on a damp towel, covered, held carefully and fed adroitly with the syringe, which is of course blunt; 2 ml is given to the fish once a day, with each feeding. Give yourself time, because the fish have difficulty swallowing. After feeding, wait 30 seconds before returning the fish to the tank, as it will swallow once more. Some of the medicine will be spat out on its being returned. Repeat the process for five days. No harm will come to the fish if it is properly handled. The medicine does no damage. This treatment will normally be sufficient, and the fish will again begin to eat. But you can easily repeat the treatment with a week in between. By this means I have saved the lives of many Discus who had stopped eating. No fish has died as a result of the treatment.

If you look very closely at the dorsal and anal fin edges, you will see fine white markings. Initially these were thought to be symptoms of a parasitic disease, but research indicated it to be just a passing phase in color changes.

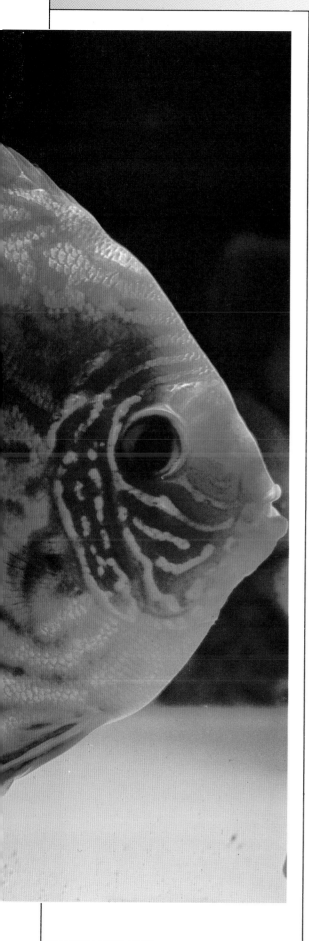

THE FUTURE

What does the future hold in store for our friend the Discus?

Will it become degraded into a mass-produced item when overseas dealers start flooding the market with colorful fish of good quality? Will Discus then still be bred only for the fast profit they can bring? We must wait and see.

Local breeders must stay true to their line and breed only high-quality specimens. Selective breeding and maintenance of the characteristics of the species, these are the things that breeders must aim for. A good shape, unflawed coloring, round, thickset specimens— these have to remain the hallmarks of home-bred Discus.

The road back to the pure-blooded wild-caught varieties must also be trod. Good purebred Brown, Green, and Blue wild-caught Discus must again be raised. They deserve greater attention. There may again be a market for the progeny of wild-caught specimens of good quality. Wild-caught progeny of this kind and the Turquoise and Royal Blue Discus in parallel would be a combination worth aiming for. Let us hope that the first small ads will soon re-appear in aquarist journals: Young Discus from wild-caught stock for sale.

The red color of this Turquoise Discus is enhanced by the light. It is, however, a very beautiful fish and one which will be enhanced by inbreeding for the future Red Discusfish. Some breeders refer to this fish as the *Red Turquoise.*

Index